KS3 Phonics

Student Workbook 2

Dear Student,

The lessons in this book will help you to improve your reading and spelling.

Learning to read and write in the English language is **super** tricky.

The English language has developed over thousands of years by different people who came to invade and live in England. This means that the modern English language contains bits of old French, Latin and Germanic languages. When people started to print books there were no rules about spelling so words were spelt in all sorts of ways. Now we have a language which is pretty complicated but very interesting. New words continue to be added to the language.

Everybody has to work hard to get better at reading and writing – even those people who seem really good at reading and spelling.

Some people think that phonics is something that we learn in the infants. We do start to learn about phonics then, but the phonic, or alphabetic, code can take many years to learn well.

Even adults who are good readers and writers still use phonics if they need to read or spell a new or difficult word.

Phonics is like a spy code.

This is a spy code: 1 = A, 2 = B, 3 = C, and so on.

Can you crack this message? (*hint: write out the alphabet in order then write the numbers 1 – 26 below it to see which letter is code for each number*)

19	16	25		3	15	4	5	19		1	18	5		1	23	5	19	15	13	5

Phonics is a code that matches the sounds that we make when we speak with the letters that we use when we read or write.

For example, when you see the letter **b** you say /b/ as in bat.

When you see the letters **ee** together you say /ee/ as in eel.

The slash marks // mean sound. The letter **c** can be a /k/ sound as in **c**at, or a /s/ sound as in **c**ity. See how it gets tricky?!

There are over 150 bits of code (letters and sounds combinations) in English so it is a lot to remember. The lessons in this book will remind you, or teach you, some of that code to help you keep the information in your long-term memory.

Contents

Some letters are preceded by a dash. The dash indicates that the letter/s – sound correspondence is not usually used at the beginning of printed words.

c(e, i, y)	g(e, i, y)	i-e	e-e
cent city cycle	gem giant gym	time	theme
o-e	a-e	u-e	air
rope	cake	cute flute	hair
-are	-ear	-ere	eer
hare	bear	where	deer
ear	-ere	-ier	ir
ears	adhere	cashier	birthday
ur	ear	(w)or	-our
nurse	earth	world	humour
-re	-le	-il	-al
theatre	kettle	pencil	hospital

-el camel	**aw** dawn	**au** sauce	**-al** chalk
oar oars	**-oor** door	**ore** snore	**-our** four
-tch patch	**-dge** fridge	**-x** exam	**kn** knot
wr write	**-mb** thumb	**sc** scissors	**gu** guitar
bu building	**ch** chameleon	**rh** rhino	**ch** chef
-ti station	**-ci** magician		

Lesson 1 c (e, i, y)

Introduction:
The letter c is code for the sound /s/ when it is followed by an e, i or y.
There are other ways to spell the sound /s/: s, -ss, -ce, -se, c (e, i, y), sc, -st- or ps.
Today we are focusing on the c (e, i, y) spelling of the /s/ sound.

1. Word reading. Read each word carefully. Tick it when you've read it.

city   cents   central   cellar   citrus   cygnet   cinema

2. Dictation time. Listen carefully and write the 3 sentences your teacher tells you.

a)

b)

c)

3. Letter hunt. Find and underline all the 'c' as /s/ code. Then read the text.

Cinderella lived in the cellar. She was a good citizen. She cooked and cleaned for her wicked step-sisters but she was never allowed out to the cinema or to the city. She felt certain that her circumstances held her back from success.

4. Now it's your turn. Write 3 short sentences that include words with today's focus code.

a)

b)

c)

5. Challenge. How do you know when the letter c may be an /s/ and not a /k/?

Lesson 2 g (e, i, y)

Introduction:
The letter g can be code for the sound /j/ when it is followed by an e, i or y.
There are other ways to spell the sound /j/: j, -dge, -ge or g (e, i, y).
Today we are focusing on the g (e, i, y) spelling of the /j/ sound.

1. Word reading. Read each word carefully. Tick it when you've read it.

gem   germ   gentle   giraffe   ginger   energy   allergy

2. Dictation time. Listen carefully and write the 3 sentences your teacher tells you.

  a)

  b)

  c)

3. Letter hunt. Find and underline all the 'g' as /j/ code. Read the text.

Gilly, the giraffe, was a gem. Ged, her keeper, explained how gentle she was. However, Gilly had an allergy to root ginger. When she was fed root ginger on Monday, she had so much energy that she jumped around like a kangaroo.

4. Now it's your turn. Write 3 short sentences that include words with today's focus code.

  a)

  b)

  c)

5. Challenge. How do you know when the letter g may be a /j/ and not a /g/?

Lesson 3 i-e as in time

Introduction:
The letters i-e are code for the sound /igh/ as in time.
There are other ways to spell the /igh/ sound too: -igh, -ie, i, -y, i-e or ei.
Today we are focusing on the i-e spelling of the /igh/ sound.

1. Word reading. Read each word carefully. Tick it when you've read it.

time   hide   like   mice   inside   mime   swiped   slime

2. Dictation time. Listen carefully and write the 3 sentences your teacher tells you.

a)
----

b)
----

c)
----

3. Letter hunt. Find and underline all the 'i-e' as /igh/ code. Then read the text.

Mike did not like mice, but he was short of time. He wiped away the breakfast mess and shined his boots. He decided to think about getting rid of the pesky mice when he got back at nine. Then he set off outside to drive away in his lime green car.

4. Now it's your turn. Write 3 short sentences that include words with today's focus code.

a)
----

b)
----

c)
----

5. Challenge. What do you notice about the 'i-e' in these words: give, live, like?

Lesson 4 e-e as in theme

Introduction:
The letters e-e are code for the sound /ee/ as in theme.
There are other ways to spell the /ee/ sound too: ee, e, e-e, -ey, -ie, ei, ea or -y.
Today we are focusing on the e-e spelling of the /ee/ sound.

1. Word reading. Read each word carefully. Tick it when you've read it.

stampede   even   theme   swede   extreme   complete

2. Dictation time. Listen carefully and write the 3 sentences your teacher tells you.

 a)
 ----
 b)
 ----
 c)
 ----

3. Letter hunt. Find and underline all the 'e-e' as /ee/ code. Then read the text.

The evening had certainly been extreme. Steve had to compete for his part in the play. A stampede of actors had completed reading the long script for the main part of the centipede. The theme of the play was the life of bugs. Steve was awarded the part.

4. Now it's your turn. Write 3 short sentences that include words with today's focus code.

 a)
 ----
 b)
 ----
 c)
 ----

5. Challenge. What do these 'e-e' words mean: concede, precede, obsolete?

Lesson 5 o-e as in rope

Introduction:
The letters o-e are code for the sound /oa/ as in rope.
There are other ways to spell the /oa/ sound too: oa, o, -oe, o-e, ow, -ough or -eau.
Today we are focusing on the o-e spelling of the /oa/ sound.

1. Word reading. Read each word carefully. Tick it when you've read it.

stone   code   throne   alone   slope   globe   smoke

2. Dictation time. Listen carefully and write the 3 sentences your teacher tells you.

 a)
----
 b)
----
 c)
----

3. Letter hunt. Find and underline all the 'o-e' as /oa/ code. Then read the text.

When Hope awoke, she was home alone. Sam rode on Sundays and Dan had sloped off out with his pals. Hope poked the embers and a little smoke rose up from the ash. She passed Jasper a bone and stroked his soft back, speaking to him in a gentle tone.

4. Now it's your turn. Write 3 short sentences that include words with today's focus code.

 a)
----
 b)
----
 c)
----

5. Challenge. What do these 'o-e' words mean: scope, abode, probe?

Lesson 6 a-e as in cake

Introduction:

The letters a-e are code for the sound /ai/ as in cake.

There are other ways to spell the /ai/ sound too: ai, ay, a, -ae, a-e, -ey, eigh, -ea or -aigh.

Today we are focusing on the a-e spelling of the /ai/ sound.

1. Word reading. Read each word carefully. Tick it when you've read it.

daze   pace   blame   graceful   shame   place   make

2. Dictation time. Listen carefully and write the 3 sentences your teacher tells you.

a)

b)

c)

3. Letter hunt. Find and underline all the 'a-e' as /ai/ code. Then read the text.

Grace was late for the start of the race. She checked her name on the list. She made her way to the start line to join the other runners. The race was held in a stunning place next to a lake. She was ashamed that she was late but was amazed when she came second!

4. Now it's your turn. Write 3 short sentences that include words with today's focus code.

a)

b)

c)

5. Challenge. What do these 'a-e' words mean: fate, instigate, infiltrate?

Lesson 7 u-e as in cute and flute

Introduction:
The letters u-e are code for the sounds /y+oo/ as in cute and /oo/ as in flute.
There are also other ways to spell these sounds.
They can both look like this: -ue, u-e or ew.
Today we are focusing on the u-e spelling of the /y+oo/ and /oo/ sounds.

1. Word reading. Read each word carefully. Tick it when you've read it.

cute rule tube salute refuse duke amused tune

2. Dictation time. Listen carefully and write the 3 sentences your teacher tells you.

a) _____

b) _____

c) _____

3. Letter hunt. Find and underline all the 'u-e' letters. Then read the text.

Duke was highly amused when Robert played the flute. "I salute your effort, Rob, but that tune is far from cute," chuckled Duke. Duke was too much of a dude to play the flute himself. "I simply refuse! I can play the tubes instead," Duke grinned.

4. Now it's your turn. Write 3 short sentences that include words with today's focus code.

a) _____

b) _____

c) _____

5. Challenge. Can you sort the words in this lesson into the two focus sounds?

_____

_____

Lesson 8 air as in hair

Introduction:
The letters air are code for the sound /air/ as in hair.
There are other ways to spell the /air/ sound too: air, -are, -ear or -ere.
Today we are focusing on the air spelling of the /air/ sound.

1. Word reading. Read each word carefully. Tick it when you've read it.

pair chair dairy despair repair stairs fair hair

2. Dictation time. Listen carefully and write the 3 sentences your teacher tells you.

a) --

b) --

c) --

3. Letter hunt. Find and underline all the 'air' as /air/ code. Then read the text.

The farmer despaired. The stairs into the dairy had not been repaired. The repairman had unfairly suggested a chairlift. The farmer sat in a chair and started to pull out his own fair hair. "This is a dairy! Just repair my stairs!" he hollered.

4. Now it's your turn. Write 3 short sentences that include words with today's focus code.

a) --

b) --

c) --

5. Challenge. What do you notice about these words: stair, stare, hair, hare?

Lesson 9 are as in hare

Introduction:
The letters are are code for the sound /air/ as in hare.
There are other ways to spell the /air/ sound too: air, -are, -ear or -ere.
Today we are focusing on the are spelling of the /air/ sound.

1. Word reading. Read each word carefully. Tick it when you've read it.

square dared compare barely spare share

2. Dictation time. Listen carefully and write the 3 sentences your teacher tells you.

a)
----
b)
----
c)
----

3. Letter hunt. Find and underline all the 'are' as /air/ code. Then read the text.

The gang was aware of the scarecrow, but they had never seen it. They were not prepared. It was late at night when they entered the farmyard. They lit a flare and waved it around at the scarecrow. It glared at them like a startled hare. They felt scared.

4. Now it's your turn. Write 3 short sentences that include words with today's focus code.

a)
----
b)
----
c)
----

5. Challenge. What do these 'are' words mean: fanfare, declare, wares?

Lesson 10 ear as in bear

Introduction:
The letters ear are code for the sound /air/ as in bear.
There are other ways to spell the /air/ sound too: air, -are, -ear or -ere.
Today we are focusing on the ear spelling of the /air/ sound.

1. Word reading. Read each word carefully. Tick it when you've read it.

swear   tear   wear   bearer   unbearable   tearing

2. Dictation time. Listen carefully and write the 3 sentences your teacher tells you.

a)
----

b)
----

c)
----

3. Letter hunt. Find and underline all the 'ear' as /air/ code. Then read the text.

Will found a tear in his best swimwear. The big race was about to start, and he had no choice but to wear the torn swimwear. The embarrassment was unbearable. The referee popped the start gun just as Will was about to swear. He dived in.

4. Now it's your turn. Write 3 short sentences that include words with today's focus code.

a)
----

b)
----

c)
----

5. Challenge. What do you notice about the words: tear, tear, bear, bare?

Lesson 11 ere as in where

Introduction:
The letters ere are code for the sound /air/ as in where.
There are other ways to spell the /air/ sound too: air, -are, -ear or -ere.
Today we are focusing on the ere spelling of the /air/ sound.

1. Word reading. Read each word carefully. Tick it when you've read it.

there where whereabouts wherever somewhere

2. Dictation time. Listen carefully and write the 3 sentences your teacher tells you.

a)

---

b)

---

c)

---

3. Letter hunt. Find and underline all the 'ere' as /air/ code. Then read the text.

The bus was stuck in traffic and the boys were getting restless.
"Where are we?" asked James.
"We are somewhere around the outskirts of Bristol," said the coach.
"When will we get there?" asked Bill. The coach sighed.

4. Now it's your turn. Write 3 short sentences that include words with today's focus code.

a)

---

b)

---

c)

---

5. Challenge. What do you notice about the words: where, ware and wear?

Lesson 12 eer as in deer

Introduction:
The letters eer are code for the sound /eer/ as in deer.
There are other ways to spell the /eer/ sound too: eer, ear, -ere or -ier.
Today we are focusing on the eer spelling of the /eer/ sound.

1. Word reading. Read each word carefully. Tick it when you've read it.

deer sneer volunteer cheer career sheer steer

2. Dictation time. Listen carefully and write the 3 sentences your teacher tells you.

a) --

b) --

c) --

3. Letter hunt. Find and underline all the 'eer' as /eer/ code. Read the text.

Edward sneered at the career advice given to him. "You suggest that I become an engineer, but I need a different steer. I think I fancy becoming a mountaineer," explained Edward. "Perhaps I shall be a volunteer. I feel cheerful when I see the deer on the hills."

4. Now it's your turn. Write 3 short sentences that include words with today's focus code.

a) --

b) --

c) --

5. Challenge. What do you notice about the words: deer and dear?

Introduction:
The letters ear are code for the sound /eer/ as in ears.
There are other ways to spell the /eer/ sound: eer, ear, -ere or -ier.
Today we are focusing on the ear spelling of the /eer/ sound.

1. Word reading. Read each word carefully. Tick it when you've read it.

hear fear appear shears nearly tearful year

2. Dictation time. Listen carefully and write the 3 sentences your teacher tells you.

a)
_____

b)
_____

c)
_____

3. Letter hunt. Find and underline all the 'ear' as /eer/ code. Read the text.

It had been nearly a year since Emily had lost the ability to hear in both ears. At the time she had appeared brave, but in fact she had felt fearful and had been in tears a lot. Now, she was used to her new life with hearing aids and she was perfectly cheerful.

4. Now it's your turn. Write 3 short sentences that include words with today's focus code.

a)
_____

b)
_____

c)
_____

5. Challenge. What do you notice about the words: hear and here?

_____

_____

Lesson 14 ere as in adhere

Introduction:
The letters ere are code for the sound /eer/ as in adhere.
There are other ways to spell the /eer/ sound: eer, ear, -ere or -ier.
Today we are focusing on the ere spelling of the /eer/ sound.

1. Word reading. Read each word carefully. Tick it when you've read it.

here   mere   interfere   persevere   sincerely   merely

2. Dictation time. Listen carefully and write the 3 sentences your teacher tells you.

a)

----

b)

----

c)

----

3. Letter hunt. Find and underline all the 'ere' as /eer/ code. Read the text.

Ravi liked to interfere in other students' lives. He never adhered to the rules. He certainly never persevered with his own projects. The teachers sincerely hoped that he would settle down but he was merely in class to fuel his social life.

4. Now it's your turn. Write 3 short sentences that include words with today's focus code.

a)

----

b)

----

c)

----

5. Challenge. What do you notice about the words: here and there?

Lesson 15 ier as in cashier

Introduction:
The letters ier are code for the sound /eer/ as in cashier.
There are other ways to spell the /eer/ sound: eer, ear, -ere or -ier.
Today we are focusing on the ier spelling of the /eer/ sound.

1. Word reading. Read each word carefully. Tick it when you've read it.

tier   pier   fierce   cashier   piercing   frontier   skier

2. Dictation time. Listen carefully and write the 3 sentences your teacher tells you.

a) _____

b) _____

c) _____

3. Letter hunt. Find and underline all the 'ier' as /eer/ code. Then read the text.

The cashier handed the money to Tanya. Tanya grinned. "Come on Sally, let's go back to the piercing shop on the pier." They went back to the piercing shop with the fierce-looking man that was covered in tattoos. "I'd like my ears pierced again," said Tanya.

4. Now it's your turn. Write 3 short sentences that include words with today's focus code.

a) _____

b) _____

c) _____

5. Challenge. What do these 'ier' words mean: cavalier, chandelier?

_____

_____

Lesson 16 ir as in birthday

Introduction:

The letters ir are code for the sound /er/ as in birthday.

There are other ways to spell the /er/ sound: er, ir, ur, ear or (w)or.

Today we are focusing on the ir spelling of the /er/ sound.

1. Word reading. Read each word carefully. Tick it when you've read it.

dirt   first   third   birthday   squirted   thirsty   stir

2. Dictation time. Listen carefully and write the 3 sentences your teacher tells you.

a) _____

b) _____

c) _____

3. Letter hunt. Find and underline all the 'ir' as /er/ code. Then read the text.

It was Miss Dirst's thirty-third birthday and she was excited about her party. Thirteen of her pals were meeting at the cinema later that evening. First, she had to visit the allotment and try not to get dirty. She was wearing a new shirt and a new skirt.

4. Now it's your turn. Write 3 short sentences that include words with today's focus code.

a) _____

b) _____

c) _____

5. Challenge. What do you notice about the words: bird, curl, earth and world?

_____

_____

Lesson 17 ur as in nurse

Introduction:
The letters ur are code for the sound /er/ as in nurse.
There are other ways to spell the /er/ sound: er, ir, ur, ear or (w)or.
Today we are focusing on the ur spelling of the /er/ sound.

1. Word reading. Read each word carefully. Tick it when you've read it.

surf   turn   burglar   murder   purse   murmur   burnt

2. Dictation time. Listen carefully and write the 3 sentences your teacher tells you.

  a)
----
  b)
----
  c)
----

3. Letter hunt. Find and underline all the 'ur' as /er/ code. Then read the text.

A surly burglar broke into the doctors' surgery just after midnight. He discovered a murder! There was a curly-haired nurse on the ground near the front desk. There was a pool of blood around her and some burnt folders by her side. The burglar went back out of the window.

4. Now it's your turn. Write 3 short sentences that include words with today's focus code.

  a)
----
  b)
----
  c)
----

5. Challenge. What do these 'ur' words mean: spurned, unfurl, murky?

Lesson 18 ear as in earth

Introduction:
The letters ear are code for the sound /er/ as in earth.
There are other ways to spell the /er/ sound: er, ir, ur, ear or (w)or.
Today we are focusing on the ear spelling of the /er/ sound.

1. Word reading. Read each word carefully. Tick it when you've read it.

earn   earth   early   pearls   search   rehearsal   heard

2. Dictation time. Listen carefully and write the 3 sentences your teacher tells you.

a)

b)

c)

3. Letter hunt. Find and underline all the 'ear' as /er/ code. Then read the text.

Pearl was obsessed with learning. She researched topics from early in the morning until late at night. She searched the Internet for facts about the earth and earls. She learned about natural and man-made pearls. She spent her earnings on books and pearls.

4. Now it's your turn. Write 3 short sentences that include words with today's focus code.

a)

b)

c)

5. Challenge. What do you notice about the words: hear and heard?

Lesson 19 (w)or as in world

Introduction:
The letters or are sometimes code for the sound /er/ when they come after a w, as in world. There are other ways to spell the /er/ sound: er, ir, ur, ear or (w)or.
Today we are focusing on the (w)or spelling of the /er/ sound.

1. Word reading. Read each word carefully. Tick it when you've read it.

worm   work   words   worst   worth   worthy   world

2. Dictation time. Listen carefully and write the 3 sentences your teacher tells you.

a) _____

b) _____

c) _____

3. Letter hunt. Find and underline all the 'or' as /er/ code. Then read the text.

William did his homework like clockwork. He stuck to the framework and he enjoyed working with words. Wendy did not. Wendy lost her passwords. She preferred to get out into the world and play with earthworms! She even went to a workshop on worms of the world.

4. Now it's your turn. Write 3 short sentences that include words with today's focus code.

a) _____

b) _____

c) _____

5. Challenge. What do you notice about the position of the 'or'?

_____

_____

Lesson 20 our as in humour

Introduction:
The letters our are code for the sound schwa /er/ (uh) as in humour.
There are other ways to spell the schwa /er/ sound: -er, -our, -re, -ar or -or.
Today we are focusing on the our spelling of the schwa /er/ sound.

1. Word reading. Read each word carefully. Tick it when you've read it.

colour   favour   rumour   honour   glamour   flavour

2. Dictation time. Listen carefully and write the 3 sentences your teacher tells you.

a)
----
b)
----
c)
----

3. Letter hunt. Find and underline all the 'our' as /er/ code. Then read the text.

Clare needed a favour. "I heard a rumour that the party will have a glamour theme. I need a different colour dress." Clare had no sense of humour when it came to fashion so I told her it was an honour to lend her a dress for the glamour party.

4. Now it's your turn. Write 3 short sentences that include words with today's focus code.

a)
----
b)
----
c)
----

5. Challenge. What do you notice about the words: glamour and glamorous?

Lesson 21 re as in theatre

Introduction:
The letters re are code for the sound schwa /er/ (uh) as in theatre.
There are other ways to spell the schwa /er/ sound: -er, -our, -re, -ar or -or.
Today we are focusing on the re spelling of the schwa /er/ sound.

1. Word reading. Read each word carefully. Tick it when you've read it.

centre   metre   litre   ogre   fibre   millimetre   acre

2. Dictation time. Listen carefully and write the 3 sentences your teacher tells you.

a)
----

b)
----

c)
----

3. Letter hunt. Find and underline all the 're' as /er/ code. Then read the text.

Dev was in a lesson but all he was thinking about was the theatre.
"How many millimetres in a kilometre?" called out the teacher.
"How many millilitres in a litre?" Dev decided that this teacher must
be an ogre. He imagined him as an ogre in a theatre show.

4. Now it's your turn. Write 3 short sentences that include words with today's focus code.

a)
----

b)
----

c)
----

5. Challenge. What do these 're' words mean: timbre, mediocre, acre?

Lesson 22 le as in kettle

Introduction:
The letters le are code for the sound /ul/ as in kettle.
There are other ways to spell the /ul/ sound: -le, -il, -al or -el.
Today we are focusing on the le spelling of the /ul/ sound.

1. Word reading. Read each word carefully. Tick it when you've read it.

niggles   sparkles   tackle   trickle   hackles   bottle

2. Dictation time. Listen carefully and write the 3 sentences your teacher tells you.

a)

----

b)

----

c)

----

3. Letter hunt. Find and underline all the 'le' as /ul/ code. Then read the text.

Little Mickey was miserable. He sat under the table in the middle of his muddled puzzle pieces, wishing he was outside with a paddle in a puddle. His sister tried to make him giggle by giving him a tickle but it just niggled him and his hackles raised.

4. Now it's your turn. Write 3 short sentences that include words with today's focus code.

a)

----

b)

----

c)

----

5. Challenge. Why do you think the /ul/ sound is spelt in different ways?

Lesson 23 il as in pencil

Introduction:
The letters il are code for the sound /ul/ as in pencil.
There are other ways to spell the /ul/ sound: -le, -il, -al or -el.
Today we are focusing on the il spelling of the /ul/ sound.

1. Word reading. Read each word carefully. Tick it when you've read it.

pupil   utensils   weevil   anvil   lentils   tonsils   April

2. Dictation time. Listen carefully and write the 3 sentences your teacher tells you.

a) _____

b) _____

c) _____

3. Letter hunt. Find and underline all the 'il' as /ul/ code. Then read the text.

It was a rainy April morning and the smell of soup was drifting down the corridor. It was lentil soup with basil that was wafting up nostrils. The clinking of utensils meant it was nearly ready. Some pupils had already started to pack up pencils and books ready to go to lunch.

4. Now it's your turn. Write 3 short sentences that include words with today's focus code.

a) _____

b) _____

c) _____

5. Challenge. What do these 'il' words mean: vigil, basil, civil?

_____

_____

Lesson 24 al as in hospital

Introduction:
The letters al are code for the sound /ul/ as in hospital.
There are other ways to spell the /ul/ sound: -le, -il, -al or -el.
Today we are focusing on the al spelling of the /ul/ sound.

1. Word reading. Read each word carefully. Tick it when you've read it.

manual   decimal   animal   several   hospital   signal

2. Dictation time. Listen carefully and write the 3 sentences your teacher tells you.

a)

---

b)

---

c)

---

3. Letter hunt. Find and underline all the 'al' as /ul/ code. Then read the text.

You must think carefully about keeping animals which need minimal care, and which are least likely to put you in hospital. How about keeping several virtual animals? They come with an online manual and make a signal like a beep when you need to tend to them.

4. Now it's your turn. Write 3 short sentences that include words with today's focus code.

a)

---

b)

---

c)

---

5. Challenge. What do these 'al' words mean: virtual, capital, final?

Lesson 25 el as in camel

Introduction:
The letters el are code for the sound /ul/ as in camel.
There are other ways to spell the /ul/ sound: -le, -il, -al or -el.
Today we are focusing on the el spelling of the /ul/ sound.

1. Word reading. Read each word carefully. Tick it when you've read it.

panel   towel   travel   jewel   kennels   parcel   label

2. Dictation time. Listen carefully and write the 3 sentences your teacher tells you.

a) --

b) --

c) --

3. Letter hunt. Find and underline all the 'el' as /ul/ code. Then read the text.

Mr Marvel was travelling home with a parcel of jewellery for his wife.
It was safely inside a gold paper towel with a small label attached.
On the way home he passed the dog kennels by the tunnel. Stuck in
traffic, he saw a lorry with an image of camels on the side panel.

4. Now it's your turn. Write 3 short sentences that include words with today's focus code.

a) --

b) --

c) --

5. Challenge. What do you notice about the position of the 'el' in words?

Lesson 26 aw as in dawn

Introduction:
The letters aw are code for the sound /or/ as in dawn.
There are other ways to spell the /or/ sound: or, ore, oar, -oor, -our, (w)ar, aw, au, -al, -augh or ough.
Today we are focusing on the aw spelling of the /or/ sound.

1. Word reading. Read each word carefully. Tick it when you've read it.

hawthorn   drawers   hawk   claws   squawk   paws

2. Dictation time. Listen carefully and write the 3 sentences your teacher tells you.

a)

b)

c)

3. Letter hunt. Find and underline all the 'aw' as /or/ code. Then read the text.

At the bottom of the lawn there is a small gap in a hawthorn bush. I can crawl into it. On the other side is a strawberry patch. The birds squawk and claw at the net over the strawberry patch but they cannot get my awesome strawberries.

4. Now it's your turn. Write 3 short sentences that include words with today's focus code.

a)

b)

c)

5. Challenge. What do these 'aw' words mean: flaw, thaw, dawning?

Introduction:
The letters au are code for the sound /or/ as in sauce.
There are other ways to spell the /or/ sound: or, ore, oar, -oor, -our, (w)ar, aw, au, -al, -augh or ough.
Today we are focusing on the au spelling of the /or/ sound.

1. Word reading. Read each word carefully. Tick it when you've read it.

applause astronaut audience author saucer

2. Dictation time. Listen carefully and write the 3 sentences your teacher tells you.

a)

----

b)

----

c)

----

3. Letter hunt. Find and underline all the 'au' as /or/ code. Then read the text.

Santa Claus and an astronaut invited an audience to a meeting. They all turned up in automobiles. The meeting's subject was 'transport'. The speaker was an author, Paul Brown. He was a staunch supporter of such meetings and launched into the subject to much applause.

4. Now it's your turn. Write 3 short sentences that include words with today's focus code.

a)

----

b)

----

c)

----

5. Challenge. What do these 'au' words mean: haul, haunches, launch?

Lesson 28 al as in chalk

Introduction:
The letters al are code for the sound /or/ as in chalk.
There are other ways to spell the /or/ sound: or, ore, oar, -oor, -our, (w)ar, aw, au, -al, -augh or ough.
Today we are focusing on the al spelling of the /or/ sound.

1. Word reading. Read each word carefully. Tick it when you've read it.

walk   stalk   small   call   stall   ball   talking   tallest

2. Dictation time. Listen carefully and write the 3 sentences your teacher tells you.

a)
----
b)
----
c)
----

3. Letter hunt. Find and underline all the 'al' as /or/ code. Then read the text.

They say 'walk tall' and I do, but it has not made me taller. I am still small. My teacher, Mr Chalk, says I am 'on the ball'. However, my grandmother says, 'pride comes before a fall'. Which goes to show that you cannot please all of the people all of the time.

4. Now it's your turn. Write 3 short sentences that include words with today's focus code.

a)
----
b)
----
c)
----

5. Challenge. What do you notice about the words: also, almost, always?

Introduction:

The letters oar are code for the sound /or/ as in oars.

There are other ways to spell the /or/ sound: or, ore, oar, -oor, -our, (w)ar, aw, au, -al, -augh or ough.

Today we are focusing on the oar spelling of the /or/ sound.

1. Word reading. Read each word carefully. Tick it when you've read it.

aboard   roar   hoard   keyboard   soar   oars   boar

2. Dictation time. Listen carefully and write the 3 sentences your teacher tells you.

a)

----

b)

----

c)

----

3. Letter hunt. Find and underline all the 'oar' as /or/ code. Then read the text.

Joan paced up and down the floorboards. She heard the wind roaring. She lifted the lid on the chest that sat on the sideboard. Inside was her hoard of gold. She scooped it into a bag, grabbed her oars and left the house. She hopped aboard her boat and smiled.

4. Now it's your turn. Write 3 short sentences that include words with today's focus code.

a)

----

b)

----

c)

----

5. Challenge. What do you notice about the words: hoarse and horse?

Lesson 30 oor as in door

Introduction:
The letters oor are code for the sound /or/ as in door.
There are other ways to spell the /or/ sound: or, ore, oar, -oor, -our, (w)ar, aw, au, -al, -augh or ough.
Today we are focusing on the oor spelling of the /or/ sound.

1. Word reading. Read each word carefully. Tick it when you've read it.

door   floor   poorly   flooring   indoors   spoor

2. Dictation time. Listen carefully and write the 3 sentences your teacher tells you.

a)

---

b)

---

c)

---

3. Letter hunt. Find and underline all the 'oor' as /or/ code. Then read the text.

Lewis felt poorly. He walked across the cold floor to get the post from the door. He looked out of the window and across the moor. He saw the boat at the mooring, but he was too poor to pay for it. He slumped into his armchair and resolved to stay indoors today.

4. Now it's your turn. Write 3 short sentences that include words with today's focus code.

a)

---

b)

---

c)

---

5. Challenge. What do you notice about the words: moor, more, poor, pour?

Lesson 31 ore as in snore

Introduction:
The letters ore are code for the sound /or/ as in snore.
There are other ways to spell the /or/ sound: or, ore, oar, -oor, -our, (w)ar, aw, au, -al, -augh or ough.
Today we are focusing on the ore spelling of the /or/ sound.

1. Word reading. Read each word carefully. Tick it when you've read it.

galore core sore bored sycamore before score

2. Dictation time. Listen carefully and write the 3 sentences your teacher tells you.

a)

---
b)

---
c)

---

3. Letter hunt. Find and underline all the 'ore' as /or/ code. Then read the text.

Jen and Dave were bored. They finished the chores and went to explore the seashore. Then they played on the swing under the sycamore tree and got some sweets from the store. They ignored Mum when she called them in before it got dark.

4. Now it's your turn. Write 3 short sentences that include words with today's focus code.

a)

---
b)

---
c)

---

5. Challenge. What do these 'ore' words mean: omnivore, herbivore?

Lesson 32 our as in four

Introduction:
The letters our are code for the sound /or/ as in four.

There are other ways to spell the /or/ sound: or, ore, oar, -oor, -our, (w)ar, aw, au, -al, -augh or ough.

Today we are focusing on the our spelling of the /or/ sound.

1. Word reading. Read each word carefully. Tick it when you've read it.

your   four   pour   court   fourth   mourn   course

2. Dictation time. Listen carefully and write the 3 sentences your teacher tells you.

a)
----

b)
----

c)
----

3. Letter hunt. Find and underline all the 'our' as /or/ code. Then read the text.

The biggest downpour in years happened on the fourth of April. Of course, it started just as Yunis was about to play in a major tennis tournament. The court was flooded in seconds. It was four days until the rain stopped.

4. Now it's your turn. Write 3 short sentences that include words with today's focus code.

a)
----

b)
----

c)
----

5. Challenge. What do you notice about the words: four, for, court, caught?

Lesson 33 tch as in patch

Introduction:
The letters tch are code for the sound /ch/ as in patch.
There is another way to spell the /ch/ sound: ch or -tch.
Today we are focusing on the tch spelling of the /ch/ sound.

1. Word reading. Read each word carefully. Tick it when you've read it.

itch hatch batch clutch ditches mismatch pitch

2. Dictation time. Listen carefully and write the 3 sentences your teacher tells you.

a)
----

b)
----

c)
----

3. Letter hunt. Find and underline all the 'tch' as /ch/ code. Then read the text.

I watched intently, almost bewitched, as my mother took a batch of hot bread rolls out of the oven. I was itching to snatch one and gobble it down with butter, but I had to wait until after the big match. When I heard the kitchen door latch I sat down in readiness.

4. Now it's your turn. Write 3 short sentences that include words with today's focus code.

a)
----

b)
----

c)
----

5. Challenge. What do these 'tch' words mean: stretcher, ditched, latches?

Lesson 34 dge as in fridge

Introduction:
The letters dge are code for the sound /j/ as in fridge.
There are other ways to spell the /j/ sound: j, -dge, -ge or g (e, i, y).
Today we are focusing on the dge spelling of the /j/ sound.

1. Word reading. Read each word carefully. Tick it when you've read it.

pledge ridge sledge wedges nudge grudge ledge

2. Dictation time. Listen carefully and write the 3 sentences your teacher tells you.

a)

---

b)

---

c)

---

3. Letter hunt. Find and underline all the 'dge' as /j/ code. Then read the text.

Hilda's lodger was a good sort. He offered to edge the hedge.
Gardening was drudgery to Hilda nowadays and the midges gave her
a hard time. In return for him edging the hedge, Hilda cooked up a
big batch of her finest fudge porridge.

4. Now it's your turn. Write 3 short sentences that include words with today's focus code.

a)

---

b)

---

c)

---

5. Challenge. What do these 'dge' words mean: sludge, drudgery, dislodge?

Lesson 35 x as in exam

Introduction:
The letter x is code for the sound /g+z/ as in exam.
The sound /g+z/ is actually two sounds /g/ and /z/ but it is useful for reading and spelling to learn as one sound unit.
Today we are focusing on the x spelling of the /g+z/ sound.

1. Word reading. Read each word carefully. Tick it when you've read it.

exam   exact   exotic   example   exit   existence

2. Dictation time. Listen carefully and write the 3 sentences your teacher tells you.

a)
----
b)
----
c)
----

3. Letter hunt. Find and underline all the 'x' as /gz/ code. Then read the text.

Emma likes exams. She finds them exhilarating. Helen thinks exams are exhausting. She exhibits signs of stress when she has to exert herself. She thinks exams exist simply to upset her. She is exactly the kind of pupil that exits the class when it is exam time.

4. Now it's your turn. Write 3 short sentences that include words with today's focus code.

a)
----
b)
----
c)
----

5. Challenge. What do these 'x' words mean: exert, exhibit, exhaust?

Lesson 36 kn as in knot

Introduction:
The letters kn are code for the sound /n/ as in knot.
There are other ways to spell the /n/ sound: n, -nn, kn, gn or -ne.
Today we are focusing on the kn spelling of the /n/ sound.

1. Word reading. Read each word carefully. Tick it when you've read it.

knee   kneel   knelt   knuckle   know   knit   knife

2. Dictation time. Listen carefully and write the 3 sentences your teacher tells you.

a)
_____

b)
_____

c)
_____

3. Letter hunt. Find and underline all the 'kn' as /n/ code. Then read the text.

Nell put down her knitting to open the door. She was shocked to see a knight kneeling in front of her clutching his knuckles. Having some knowledge about healing, Nell took him inside. His cut had been inflicted with a hunting knife.

4. Now it's your turn. Write 3 short sentences that include words with today's focus code.

a)
_____

b)
_____

c)
_____

5. Challenge. What do you notice about the position of the 'kn' in words?

_____

_____

Introduction:

The letters wr are code for the sound /r/ as in write.

There are other ways to spell the /r/ sound: r, -rr, wr or rh.

Today we are focusing on the wr spelling of the /r/ sound.

1. Word reading. Read each word carefully. Tick it when you've read it.

wrap   wreck   wrist   wrinkle   wrapping   written

2. Dictation time. Listen carefully and write the 3 sentences your teacher tells you.

a)

----

b)

----

c)

----

3. Letter hunt. Find and underline all the 'wr' as /r/ code. Then read the text.

Tabitha was a writer. She put on her wrap and opened her front door. She wrinkled her nose at the wind and wrangled with the plan to go for a walk. She was glad when she did go out as she saw a wren down by the shipwreck on the beach.

4. Now it's your turn. Write 3 short sentences that include words with today's focus code.

a)

----

b)

----

c)

----

5. Challenge. What do you notice about the position of the 'wr' in words?

Introduction:
The letters mb are code for the sound /m/ as in thumb.
There are other ways to spell the /m/ sound: m, -mm, -me, -mb or mn.
Today we are focusing on the mb spelling of the /m/ sound.

1. Word reading. Read each word carefully. Tick it when you've read it.

lamb limb numb bomb thumb climb plumber

2. Dictation time. Listen carefully and write the 3 sentences your teacher tells you.

a)

----

b)

----

c)

----

3. Letter hunt. Find and underline all the 'mb' as /m/ code. Then read the text.

Jayden was a hard-working plumber. One day he was rushing when he climbed his ladder. He stumbled and trapped his thumb in a door jamb, and he broke a limb. He felt dumb as he sat at home afterwards. He sat meekly like a little lamb.

4. Now it's your turn. Write 3 short sentences that include words with today's focus code.

a)

----

b)

----

c)

----

5. Challenge. What do these 'mb' words mean: succumb, comb, tomb?

Lesson 39 sc as in scissors

Introduction:
The letters sc are code for the sound /s/ as in scissors.
There are other ways to spell the /s/ sound: s, -ss, -ce, -se, c (e, i, y), sc, -st- or ps.
Today we are focusing on the sc spelling of the /s/ sound.

1. Word reading. Read each word carefully. Tick it when you've read it.

scent   scissors   scene   scientist   scythe   science

2. Dictation time. Listen carefully and write the 3 sentences your teacher tells you.

a)
_____

b)
_____

c)
_____

3. Letter hunt. Find and underline all the 'sc' as /s/ code. Then read the text.

The scientist was on his way back from a science conference. The sun was setting, and it was a stunning scene from the train window. An old farmer was using a scythe to trim the meadow grass. The scent of wild-flowers filled the air and crept in at the top of the window.

4. Now it's your turn. Write 3 short sentences that include words with today's focus code.

a)
_____

b)
_____

c)
_____

5. Challenge. What do you notice about the position of the 'sc' in words?

_____

_____

Lesson 40 gu as in guitar

Introduction:
The letters gu are code for the sound /g/ as in guitar.
There are other ways to spell the /g/ sound: g, -gg, gu, gh or -gue.
Today we are focusing on the gu spelling of the /g/ sound.

1. Word reading. Read each word carefully. Tick it when you've read it.

guess   guest   guard   guilty   guide   disguise   guy

2. Dictation time. Listen carefully and write the 3 sentences your teacher tells you.

a)
----

b)
----

c)
----

3. Letter hunt. Find and underline all the 'gu' as /g/ code. Then read the text.

The guard watched the guest carrying a guitar out of the hotel. He wondered if this was the guy that he had been told to look out for. Were the dark glasses and beard a disguise? The guy looked so ordinary no one guessed that he was guilty.

4. Now it's your turn. Write 3 short sentences that include words with today's focus code.

a)
----

b)
----

c)
----

5. Challenge. What do you notice about the position of the 'gu' in words?

Lesson 41 bu as in building

Introduction:
The letters bu are code for the sound /b/ as in building.
There are other ways to spell the /b/ sound: b, -bb or bu.
Today we are focusing on the bu spelling of the /b/ sound.

1. Word reading. Read each word carefully. Tick it when you've read it.

buy   buyer   buoy   buoyant   builder   building

2. Dictation time. Listen carefully and write the 3 sentences your teacher tells you.

a)

----

b)

----

c)

----

3. Letter hunt. Find and underline all the 'bu' as /b/ code. Then read the text.

Nothing could compare with the buoyant feelings the builder felt when looking at the magnificent building he had built. Except, perhaps, the builder's feelings when he sold the building to an equally jubilant buyer.

4. Now it's your turn. Write 3 short sentences that include words with today's focus code.

a)

----

b)

----

c)

----

5. Challenge. What do you notice about the position of the 'bu' in words?

Lesson 42 ch as in chameleon

Introduction:
The letters ch can be code for the sound /k/ as in chameleon.
There are other ways to spell the /k/ sound: k, c, -ck, ch, qu or que.
Today we are focusing on the ch spelling of the /k/ sound.

1. Word reading. Read each word carefully. Tick it when you've read it.

school   chorus   chemist   character   chronic   cholera

2. Dictation time. Listen carefully and write the 3 sentences your teacher tells you.

a)

----

b)

----

c)

----

3. Letter hunt. Find and underline all the 'ch' as /k/ code. Then read the text.

It was just before Christmas. Characters needed to be picked for the school play. Decisions needed to be made for the school chorus. An outbreak of cholera had caused complete chaos and school had be abandoned while the chemist battled chronic ailments.

4. Now it's your turn. Write 3 short sentences that include words with today's focus code.

a)

----

b)

----

c)

----

5. Challenge. What other sounds are represented by the letters 'ch'?

Lesson 43 rh as in rhino

Introduction:
The letters rh are code for the sound /r/ as in rhino.
There are other ways to spell the /r/ sound: r, -rr, wr or rh.
Today we are focusing on the rh spelling of the /r/ sound.

1. Word reading. Read each word carefully. Tick it when you've read it.

rhubarb rhino rhombus rhymes rhetoric rhythm

2. Dictation time. Listen carefully and write the 3 sentences your teacher tells you.

a)
----
b)
----
c)
----

3. Letter hunt. Find and underline all the 'rh' as /r/ code. Then read the text.

Ronnie Rhinoceros and Rita Rhebok were great pals. They both loved to eat rhubarb and do the rhumba. They were very into rhythm and rhetoric of the rhyming kind. Rita wore rhinestones and Ronnie danced to rhapsodies by the rhododendrons.

4. Now it's your turn. Write 3 short sentences that include words with today's focus code.

a)
----
b)
----
c)
----

5. Challenge. What do these 'rh' words mean: rhapsody, rhebok, rhinestone?

Lesson 44 ch as in chef

Introduction:
The letters ch can also be code for the sound /sh/ as in chef.
There are other ways to spell the /sh/ sound: sh, ch, -ti, -ci or -ssi.
Today we are focusing on the ch spelling of the /sh/ sound.

1. Word reading. Read each word carefully. Tick it when you've read it.

chiffon   chute   chaperone   machine   charades

2. Dictation time. Listen carefully and write the 3 sentences your teacher tells you.

a)

---
b)

---
c)

---

3. Letter hunt. Find and underline all the 'ch' as /sh/ code. Then read the text.

Shaun was a successful young chef, but he was a show-off. He loved to brag about his parent' posh chalet with its crystal chandeliers. One day he decided his shoes needed a shine. He put them in the washing machine with his mum's best chiffon shirts.

4. Now it's your turn. Write 3 short sentences that include words with today's focus code.

a)

---
b)

---
c)

---

5. Challenge. What do these 'ch' words mean: chivalry, chassis, chalet?

Lesson 45 ti as in station

Introduction:
The letters ti can be code for the sound /sh/ as in station.
There are other ways to spell the /sh/ sound: sh, ch, -ti, -ci or -ssi.
Today we are focusing on the ti spelling of the /sh/ sound.

1. Word reading. Read each word carefully. Tick it when you've read it.

nation   motion   station   patient   partial   essential

2. Dictation time. Listen carefully and write the 3 sentences your teacher tells you.

a)

----

b)

----

c)

----

3. Letter hunt. Find and underline all the 'ti' as /sh/ code. Then read the text.

As a nation, it is essential that we take action and put forward a motion to address the torrential rainfall. Initially we waited patiently to see developments in the weather patterns. However, this situation needs to be treated with urgency.

4. Now it's your turn. Write 3 short sentences that include words with today's focus code.

a)

----

b)

----

c)

----

5. Challenge. What do you notice about the position of the 'ti' in words?

Lesson 46 ci as in magician

Introduction:
The letters ci can also be code for the sound /sh/ as in magician.
There are other ways to spell the /sh/ sound: sh, ch, -ti, -ci or -ssi.
Today we are focusing on the ci spelling of the /sh/ sound.

1. Word reading. Read each word carefully. Tick it when you've read it.

official   special   musician   ancient   artificial

2. Dictation time. Listen carefully and write the 3 sentences your teacher tells you.

 a)
 ----
 b)
 ----
 c)
 ----

3. Letter hunt. Find and underline all the 'ci' as /sh/ code. Then read the text.

Patience was making a special cake following an ancient recipe. She needed to buy an essential ingredient. Her mother looked with suspicion at the list of ingredients. "Artificial food colouring would not be in an official ancient recipe," she said.

4. Now it's your turn. Write 3 short sentences that include words with today's focus code.

 a)
 ----
 b)
 ----
 c)
 ----

5. Challenge. What do you notice about the position of the 'ci' in words?

Lesson 47 Word level assessment

1. Word reading. Read and tick the words.

cinema	vertical	nowhere	niggles	third
spurned	gentle	research	career	prawns
scraped	launch	crime	flannel	nearly
weevil	amused	litre	swede	chalk
sincere	board	flair	ignore	throne
flavour	cavalier	emotion	declare	worst

2. Word dictation. Listen and write the words.

1.	2.	3.	4.	5.
6.	7.	8.	9.	10.
11.	12.	13.	14.	15.
16.	17.	18.	19.	20.
21.	22.	23.	24.	25.
26.	27.	28.	29.	30.

1. Read the passage.

It was the start of the autumn term and all the students pledged to try their best. Despite good intentions, things soon turned crazy. Susan had an allergic reaction to a science experiment. An ambulance had to be sent to take her to hospital. Students gathered around to watch the unfolding scene. Next a large number of staff came down with a terrible tickle in their throats. They blamed the onset of cold and damp weather which had been long overdue after a sweltering summer. The registers got muddled and teachers called students by the wrong surnames. By the third week of term everybody needed a holiday. Instead they had to start play rehearsals if they wanted to be ready by Christmas. At least the new school website was launched successfully so virtual guests could increase their knowledge of the school and its policies.

2. Listen and write.

The English Alphabetic Code Chart

sounds	simple code	complex code (spelling alternatives)						
/s/	s snake	-ss glass	-ce palace	-se house	c (e i y) city	sc scissors	-st- castle	ps pseudonym
/a/	a apple							
/t/	t tent	-tt letter	-ed skipped					
/i/	i insect	-y cymbals						
/p/	p pan	-pp puppet						
/n/	n net	-nn bonnet	kn knot	gn gnome	-ne engine			
/k/	k kit	c cat	-ck duck	ch chameleon	qu bouquet	que plaque		
/e/	e egg	-ea head	ai said					
/h/	h hat	wh who						
/r/	r rat	-rr arrow	wr write	rh rhinoceros				
/m/	m map	-mm hammer	-me welcome	-mb thumb	-mn column			
/d/	d dig	-dd puddle	-ed rained					
/g/	g girl	-gg juggle	gu guitar	gh ghost	-gue catalogue			
/o/	o octopus	(w)a watch	(qu)a qualify	a(lt) salt				
/u/	u umbrella	o son	-ou touch	-ough thorough				
/l/	l ladder	-ll shell						
/ul/	-le kettle	-il pencil	-al hospital	-el camel				
/f/	f feather	-ff cliff	ph photograph	-gh laugh				
/b/	b bat	-bb rabbit	bu building					
/j/	j jug	-ge cabbage	g (e i y) giraffe	-dge Fridge				
/y/	y yawn							
/ai/	ai aid	-ay tray	a table	-ae sundae	a-e cake			
	-ey prey	-ea break	eigh eight	-aigh straight				
/w/	w web	wh wheel	-u penguin					
/oa/	oa oak	ow bow	o yo-yo	-oe oboe	o-e rope	-ough dough	eau plateau	

/igh/	-igh night	-ie tie	i behind	-y fly	i-e bike	ei eider	eye eye	
/ee/	ee eel	ea eat	e emu	e-e concrete	-ey key	-ie chief	-i(ne) sardine	
/i-ee/	-y sunny	-ey monkey	-ie movie					
/or/	or fork	oar oars	-oor door	ore snore	-our four	(w)ar wardrobe	(qu)ar quarter	(w)a water
	aw dawn	au sauce	-al chalk	-augh caught	ough thought			
/z/	z zebra	-zz jazz	-s fries	-se cheese	-ze breeze			
/ng/	-ng gong	-n jungle		/ngk/	-nk ink	-nc uncle		
/v/	v violin	-ve dove						
short /oo/	-oo book	-oul should	-u push					
long /oo/	oo moon	-ue blue	u-e flute	-ew crew	-ui fruit	-ou soup	-o move	-ough through
/ks/	-x fox	-ks books	-cks ducks	-kes cakes		/gz/	-x exam	-gs pegs
/ch/	ch chairs	-tch patch		/chu/	-ture picture			
/sh/	sh sheep	ch chef	-ti station	-ci magician	-ssi admission			
unvoiced /th/	th thistle		voiced /th/	th there				
/kw/	qu queen							
/ou/	ou ouch	ow owl	-ough plough					
/oi/	oi ointment	oy toy						
/yoo/	-ue statue	u unicorn	u-e tube	ew new	eu pneumatic			
/er/	er mermaid	ir birthday	ur nurse	ear earth	(w)or world			
schwa /er/ (uh)	-er mixer	-our humour	-re theatre	-ar collar	-or sailor			
/ar/	ar artist	a father	al(m) palm	-al(f) half	-al(ves) calves			
/air/	air hair	-are hare	-ear bear	-ere where				
/eer/	eer deer	ear ears	-ere adhere	-ier cashier				
/zh/	-si television	-s treasure	-z azure	g courgette	-ge collage			

(Shaded grapheme boxes indicate coverage in this workbook)

55

First published by Blackberry Cottage Ltd, UK 2019-09-06

Print ISBN: 978-1691505098

www.abigailsteel.com

With credit, acknowledgement and thanks to Debbie Hepplewhite, MBE.
www.alphabeticcodecharts.com
www.phonicsinternational.com

With thanks to Academies Enterprise Trust for their forward thinking, inclusive approaches and passion for children to choose remarkable lives.

With thanks to the dedicated and hard-working staff at Clacton Coastal Academy who inspired this curriculum and will lead change by implementing it with their students.

Printed in Great Britain
by Amazon

37332020R00033

Eating Curry for Heaven's Sake!

Creative Christian Interfaith Engagement

Barbara Glasson

kevin
mayhew

kevin mayhew

First published in Great Britain in 2015 by Kevin Mayhew Ltd
Buxhall, Stowmarket, Suffolk IP14 3BW
Tel: +44 (0) 1449 737978 Fax: +44 (0) 1449 737834
E-mail: info@kevinmayhew.com

www.kevinmayhew.com

9 8 7 6 5 4 3 2 1 0

ISBN 978 1 84867 791 3
Catalogue No. 1501487

Cover design and layout by Rob Mortonson
© Images used under licence from Shutterstock Inc.
Edited by Virginia Rounding

Printed and bound in Great Britain

TOUCHSTONE
listening for a change

Contents

Introduction

My name is Barbara Glasson and I am the Team Leader at Touchstone, a church-based community project in the centre of Bradford, West Yorkshire. I am a Methodist Minister who has had to learn a lot about interfaith engagement during the last six years. This book is intended for Christians who are embarking on a similar journey or are perplexed by issues, or feel out of their depth or think that multiculturalism is not their concern . . . in reality, that's most of us!

I am writing out of Bradford's context, aware that where you are will be significantly different. I am referring mostly to engagement with Muslims of Pakistani heritage, not the usual mix of multiculturalism found in other British cities. I am writing for Christians. I make no apology for any of this bias – what's important is for this book to help give you the confidence to engage where you are, however that looks or feels.

When I write about 'Christians' or 'Muslims', 'White British people' or 'people of Pakistani heritage', I am not referring to homogenous groupings of humanity but rather to a complex and nuanced variety of people with differing groups, opinions and allegiances within each 'group'. And history isn't monochrome either; a Muslim from Turkey will have a significantly different cultural and religious heritage from one from Pakistan – we all have baggage! Just as there is no such thing as an 'ordinary Christian', so there is no such thing as 'a Muslim' or 'a Sikh'. Within each faith tradition are many different theologies, so I apologise if I have generalised too much at times, but this is a small book and there are plenty of more complex tomes that can further deepen understanding.

Whilst I want to encourage all of us to engage and learn and grow and flourish in the rich intercultural mix of our society, I don't want to ignore some of the deeper and harder questions which arise when we engage with people holding different beliefs and cultures from our own. There are some hard issues out there, and we need safe space to engage with them. I hope that this book will be used by groups of people who can create safe enough space for such rigorous discussion. I hope that, in such honest dialogue, we won't simply talk about what we *think* but also how we *feel*. I trust there will be sufficient wisdom to allow this conversation to flow into deeper understanding all round. And I hope that some of the suggestions at the end of each chapter will not simply be personal challenges but will also inform group and church engagement so that we can own our interfaith journey *together*.

This is a short and, I hope, simple book, but also a doorway to further learning. There are some suggestions for further reading and viewing at the end of the book, but dip into them at any time as your interest is stirred.

Interfaith engagement is not a specialist activity, it is part of our Christian vocation; after all, our Jesus was born into the context of religious and cultural diversity. Not only will such exploration lead to fruitful and lasting transformation of communities, it will also strengthen our own beliefs as we find what is precious to us in new ways. There was never a more important time for us to be faith literate and to talk of the incarnate God who loves the world deeply enough to send Jesus. We are:

Eating CURRY FOR Heaven's sake!

Samosa- small beginnings

The samosa, a deep-fried triangular pastry filled with highly-spiced meat or vegetables, originating in the Middle East. Variations have spread as far and wide as South East Asia and Africa.

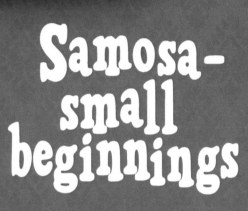

This is street food at its finest, freshly cooked in huge cauldrons of boiling oil on every corner across the sub-continent and beyond, eaten on the move, sometimes with a simple side dish of spiced chickpeas or a salad fashioned from coriander and onion.

Six years ago I moved to be the Methodist Minister in the centre of Bradford. Although all my ministry has been in urban contexts, this was the first time I encountered being in a Christian minority in a majority Muslim city. For the first year of my new appointment, as the Team Leader at a project called Touchstone, I relished the feeling of being in a new culture – and that was just Yorkshire! Most of my neighbours are from the Mirpur region of Pakistan, an area near the border with Kashmir. These people of Pakistani heritage had however mostly lived in Bradford longer than me, had assimilated into the city and spoke with broad Yorkshire accents. I enjoyed visiting the Bombay stores and picking up a bargain and frequenting the Asian supermarket up the road where it was possible to buy paratha and cheap lentils – and then, of course, there are the restaurants!

Bradford is the curry capital of England and hosts a world-famous Curry Festival once a year. The flavours and aromas of spices and herbs exude out of many Bradford letter boxes and nowhere is more aromatic than Great Horton Road or Leeds Road where the restaurant owners make a curry mile, or two. Most of us white indigenous Brits talk of eating Asian food as 'going for an Indian', but it is Pakistan's rich history and heritage that influence the **menu of most Bradford restaurants, and often the chef is Bangladeshi!**

In 2013 I made my first trip to Pakistan, to help with some clergy training in the Church of Pakistan. It was like being shown the other side of a coin, and what struck me most were the stereotypes I had been holding about what Pakistan would be like. I had visited India in the past and had a notion that Pakistan would be just the same but a bit further north! My ignorance astounded me when I visited a museum in Lahore and saw a vast array of coins that had been found in archaeological digs in the country. Coins from the Middle East, from Afghanistan, from China and, of course, from India adorned the display. Pakistan is on most of the ancient trade routes of the world and has a rich and varied cultural and architectural history. It also has a new history since partition from India and has distinctive geographical significance due to its proximity to Afghanistan, China, Russia and the Middle East.

Returning to Bradford, I realised that my rather feeble attempts at interfaith dialogue were of the 'curry and quiche' variety. That is, as a faith leader in the city I was being invited to various civic functions where we ate — well, famously, soup and samosa — and made polite conversation with others considered to be similar representatives of various faiths. These gatherings were by and large initiated by members of the City Council with an 'inclusion' agenda, intent on keeping civic peace and community cohesion but often without any real understanding of the part that faith can play if allowed to inform real and honest conversations beyond the curry and quiche variety.

At the same time I was having conversations with members of churches in other places, good people glad that we were 'doing' interfaith in Bradford so that they wouldn't have to: after all, 'We don't have that problem here.' What I want to do in this writing is to say why interfaith and intercultural conversation is crucial not only in a city such as Bradford, but even in little rural hamlets without an obvious cultural or faith mix — and why we need to get beyond the curry and quiche. In order to do so, I am taking a number of Asian dishes and using them as starting points for understanding our theology of diversity. Then there will be some suggestions for further reading, films and YouTube videos to enable individuals or groups to make a start in their interfaith understanding. And finally, each chapter will conclude with a recipe of some yummy dish to enable a group to have round-table conversations in a warm and conducive atmosphere.

The intention is that anyone should be able to begin to expand their horizons and think more creatively about people of other faiths. And that, in the process, the word 'interfaith' will stop being something for experts who know how to leap the great ravine between faiths, but will instead come to represent an everyday exploration of what it means for all of us to live in multicultural Britain.

I also want to stress that 'interfaith dialogue' is not an optional extra to the understanding of our faith, but a key part of understanding ourselves as Christians in Britain today. There is great joy and wonder in such an exploration, and also a number of fears to be faced and overcome. So go on, I dare you, jump in!

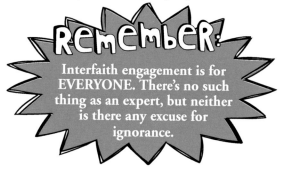

REMEMBER!

Interfaith engagement is for EVERYONE. There's no such thing as an expert, but neither is there any excuse for ignorance.

Don't try making Samosa yet, just pop into your nearest Asian corner shop, or find the World Food aisle in the supermarket or your nearest takeaway. You'll not only have a great meal, but also possibly your first interfaith conversation — see, it's easier than you thought!

Korma - beginning gently

A korma is very often seen as the poor relation of the curry pantheon, a mild curry for people who don't really like curry.

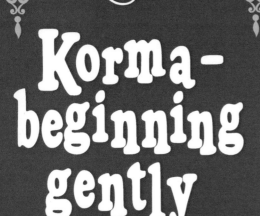

It originated in the grand courts of the Moghul Empire in the sixteenth or seventeenth century as a feast dish, a party or banquet dish for a very special occasion, made with the very best ingredients and plenty of expensive and top-quality spices. A true korma isn't bland, and it doesn't deserve the reputation it's got . . . instead, it's a rich and opulent dish with a hint of luxury about it.

My hunch is that most of us do not think of korma as a dish of rich flavours originating from the Mughal dynasty but rather as a safe option on a menu. The sort of choice if we are unsure of the spice levels of other dishes. Something fairly bland we know and can manage. It's where most of us start with interfaith encounters: 'What's safe?'

So let's begin this gastronomic discourse by celebrating the joy of intercultural engagement offered by this simple dish, because even the simplest of intercultural engagement is marinated in the history of the world. I live and work in Bradford, but it was only when I visited Pakistan for the first time that I realised what rich history had moved into my street. Pakistan is on many ancient trade routes of the world. Cradled between Afghanistan and India, it borders China and the Middle East. People have walked or marched across its borders before it even had any. Traders and dynasties have walked, or ridden elephants across the land, princes and war lords have come and gone, and continue to come and go. Pakistan has three deserts and high mountains, its citizens speak different languages. The architecture and the art reflect all this rich history – domed mosques with Moroccan-style tiles, the Sufi shrines of Multan, the grey-eyed children of Peshawar.

And of course, the history of Pakistan is peppered with the flavours of the British: from the railway system to the medium of instruction, England and Pakistan are inextricably linked. It is this history and this background and culture that are reflected on the streets of Bradford and that pervade the joyful complexity of multiculturalism.

So let's dispel the notion that the korma curry is for wimps. Here is the starting point for interfaith learning, handed to us on a plate with this simple, rich, complex and interesting dish.

Whether you're venturing out on your first korma curry, or you're already a hard-core chilli-biting curry freak, the chances are that you're eating in a Pakistani rather than an Indian restaurant, and the chef could have come from anywhere in South Asia. The migration of people from the Asian sub-continent to the UK is one of the more noticeable influxes of recent years, and links us to our own industrial history. In the case of West Yorkshire, Pakistani men were invited to work in the woollen mills, because they had particular skills with the machinery that was being used. During the 1960s these migrant workers set up in households together – working in shifts and sharing bedrooms and food.

> It's where most of us start with interfaith encounters: 'What's safe?'

Pakistan

that we don't extrapolate what we perceive in one person to prove a point about a whole race. Some Pakistanis speak English, others don't; some will shake your hand when you meet, others won't; some will be Muslim, but not all. People see that I am British and assume that I am not friendly, love fish and chips and agree with David Cameron (only one of these is true, and it's fattening!). We are only racist if we use these assumptions to restrict the rights of someone else to deviate from our assumed racial norms.

SO the FIRSt STep is to SmILe and SaY heLLo.

The intention was to work hard and send money home to Pakistan, and in time to return themselves. In Bradford this infux was from a very few villages on the border with Kashmir, in Mirpur. Different cities will have different links with our colonial and industrial histories. It is wrong to think that people from South Asia come as strangers – our histories are intimately linked, from Raj to restaurant.

The reason for beginning in this rich diet of history is to remind us that we are not receiving strangers to Britain, but rather people with whom we share national and international history. We are also receiving people with a rich history of their own, as anyone who has read about the partition of India will appreciate. But that is not to say that we don't feel the strangeness of migrant communities moving into our neighbourhoods or that there aren't challenges associated with whole communities changing their ethnic mix. And if we are fearful of engagement, these fears are born out of a real sense of perplexity.

Let me name some of these fears, because in naming them we can begin to identify some of the strategies for managing them. The first fear is probably that we are frightened of being considered racist. Here we are not always helped by a sense that we ought to be 'politically correct'. The truth is that we notice people of different colour or who are speaking a different language and it makes us feel perplexed. How are we to greet people, what if they don't speak English, what if we offend them in some way? So, let's be clear – we all identify people by their race, and make assumptions based on this assessment. The important thing is

Don't be offended if someone rejects your outstretched hand, and ask some open questions about family or the weather. Get over feeling a bit silly if someone doesn't speak English. And acknowledge your inner racist and notice what feels difficult. Remember that you are also being identified by your race, and be resistant to any assumptions being made about you as well.

The second fear may be that of feeling ignorant. So let's be quite clear about this – there is no such thing as an expert in interfaith. True, there are scholars, and there are theologians and there are people that live in different cultures and have accumulated knowledge born of first-hand experience. And to be honest, there are also people who blag quite well. Some may know more than we do, but they are not interfaith experts, because the ground is always changing, the political situation is complex and faiths are not monochrome but nuanced with a wide variety of interpretation. So don't be intimidated! There is no such thing as a daft question.

The biggest excuse for feeling ignorant is that 'there are no ethnic minorities where I live'. But that is no reason at all for not being engaged with intercultural issues. Whether we live in Bradford or Bodmin, we still inhabit the same international landscape. We see the same news on our TV screens and we are part of the same nation and political system.

WE ARE ALL INVOLVED WITH WELCOMING STRANGERS AND 'NEWCOMERS' INTO OUR COMMUNITIES, WHETHER THEY COME FROM BANGLADESH OR BRISTOL.

Many people with negative views of ethnic diversity have fled the urban environment and inhabit some pretend rural idyll somewhere on a train line to work. The most important place for interfaith dialogue may consequently be out in rural or suburban contexts where people have perhaps closed their minds to the importance of diversity by imagining: 'we don't have that problem here'.

SO EVEN IF YOU FEEL IGNORANT, YOU REALLY HAVE NO EXCUSE FOR REMAINING SO.

The third fear might be that we are frightened of being converted or overwhelmed or put on the spot. All of us are happier being in like-minded communities, either where we live or in our virtual online worlds. We choose to inhabit spaces where people agree with us or our deeply held beliefs are confirmed. It's much more comfortable to be in a faith community that has a shared set of beliefs, than to engage with others who might make us doubt what is true. We can be scared of people who might 'out argue' us or put us on the spot about what we actually believe.

This happened to me recently at Islamabad airport when a certain taxi driver from Dewsbury asked me if I could sum up in three minutes why I was a Christian. When push came to shove, I declared that it was because the Christian faith was the only world religion with the imperative to love our enemies and pray for those who persecute us, and it was by this imperative that I chose to live my life! When I got back to Bradford, I fell to wondering whether Christianity was in fact the only religion to instruct us in this love of enemies (it is), and I realised that I had work to do on my own faith understanding if I wanted to feel more robust when put on the

spot. We Christians are a bit lazy when it comes to working out what we actually believe. If we are afraid of being challenged, then we have work to do to make sure we know why we are Christian. This sort of faith resilience will enable us to engage openly and warmly with others without fear of being overwhelmed. So, there is work to be done! To really engage with interfaith conversations, we need to be confident about who we are and then we can be open to listening to what other people believe without fear.

And the last fear I want to name is that of being misunderstood. We white British tend to be very . . . well, very British. We are disconcerted when we don't understand the social conventions of another set of people and we easily withdraw into our introverted and conventional worlds. Added to this, we have a lot of our post-colonial baggage to unpack as well as our views and experiences concerning recent conflicts in the Middle East and Afghanistan. In short, we have history. And because of this we get to feel nervous, not least as Christians. We are no longer the confident missional nation that had the security of faith and empire on our side, nor are we currently conflict free. We are not sure how to interpret our involvement with people and churches in other lands, not to mention our history with other faiths, from crusades to 'axes of evil' and we are fearful of being either too dominant or too submissive in relation to our international and local neighbours. It is true that our political history is both convoluted and complex and that we are perplexed by whether our politicians have acted justly or repressively. We become anxious about how our local actions will be interpreted – are we being imperialistic? Are we assuming a colonial supremacy? So this anxiety can trip us up, and we are led to a default position of keeping our heads down.

Here then are the fears I have identified:

- Fear of being considered racist

- Fear of feeling ignorant

- Fear of being overwhelmed

- Fear of being misunderstood

And now we have put all that on the table, let's get real and opt into interfaith encounter because, on the whole, we are going to learn a lot more and be more enriched than we could ever imagine. Korma may be mild, but it is not bland, and from it we begin to appreciate the wonderfully rich flavours of another heritage and culture. It was from just such a nuanced interfaith environment that our faith was born. Christians finding their way within Judaism; religious minorities finding their voice in occupied lands; marginalised, struggling people being able to speak truth to power: it's what Jesus was about.

Questions to ask yourself:

- If I am honest, what are my fears about interfaith engagement?

- In the light of this chapter, can I identify any occasions when I have experienced or spoken racist comments?

- What assumptions do I make about people of other cultures that I might want to change?

- What stops me voicing my fears about people with different beliefs from my own?

- Is there anywhere I feel safe to talk about these things? If there is, what makes it feels safe? If there isn't, how could I make one?

Practical things to do:

- Pop into a welcome centre for asylum seekers or refugees.

- Have a chat with your Asian taxi driver or waiter, doctor or school friend about . . . anything!

- In a TV programme or soap that you watch, see how religious characters are portrayed and ask: is this positive or negative?

- Watch a film or read a book and share it with others in a group. (For a starter see recommendations at the end of this book.)

- Remember to pray for people who have another faith, both privately and in Sunday worship.

- Try to be a better listener!

- Visit an unfamiliar place of worship and see what surprises you.

Recipe: Chicken Korma

3 tbsp natural yoghurt
1½ tsp red chilli powder
1½ tsp salt (or to taste)
1 tsp garam masala
1 medium onion – finely chopped
8 tbsp oil
Whole spices: 1 or 2 cardamom
2 x 2" pieces of cinnamon stick
1½ tsp cumin seeds
6 cloves
1 garlic clove – finely chopped
1" fresh ginger – finely chopped
1kg chicken on the bone (could use chicken fillets)
2 green chillies – chopped
Fresh coriander – chopped
Water

STORY:

Rukshana teaches both Urdu and cookery at Bradford College. Although she has been in the UK since her marriage, she still misses her mother's cooking back in Pakistan. She uses traditional recipes in her classes and tries to adapt them for British taste.

Although Rukshana's favourite dish is biryani, she has contributed a korma to this book. Unlike most korma recipes, hers is an original one and contains no coconut – she says that when it is cooked it should be a 'good dark colour'. Rukshana is a very patient teacher; she has a class of mixed ability students, mostly of South Asian heritage who are learning Urdu which is considered a more refined language than Punjabi.

1. In a mixing bowl, add the yoghurt, chilli powder, salt and garam masala. Mix thoroughly and set aside.

2. Fry the onion in oil until golden brown.

3. Now add the whole spices and fry for 2 minutes.

4. Add the ginger and garlic and fry for another 2 minutes.

5. Add the chicken and cook for 3-4 minutes.

6. Add the yoghurt paste to the chicken and fry for 5-6 minutes until the oil separates.

7. Now add the green chillies whole, with the coriander. Add ¼ pint of water and simmer for 1-2 minutes. Then put the lid on and continue to simmer on low heat for 3-4 minutes until it's cooked. Serve with roti (see next chapter) or rice.

REMEMBER:

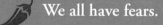

🌶 We all have fears.

🌶 There's no such thing as a daft question.

🌶 Jesus lived in an interfaith world too!

Roti – stories that unite

The roti is the staple bread of the South Asian region. It's bread in its simplest form, nothing more than a mix of wholemeal flour, a little salt, and water, kneaded and stretched into flat pancakes and cooked on a fiercely hot and blackened iron pan called a tawa until it blisters and cracks. Rotis carry the role of accompaniment, cutlery and plate in one.

It is important in our discovery of interfaith engagement to remember that we begin with a shared story and this is no better illustrated than in the story of bread. For the Abrahamic traditions – 'The People of the Book' – there is a special shared history that comes from the rich stories and insights of the Hebrew Bible. In Judaism 'Lechem' was such an important element of the diet that this word for bread was sometimes used to describe food in general.

Making grain offerings with unleavened loaves would be a feature of the offerings in the temple.

When baking large amounts of bread, the Jewish law requires that a small portion be set aside and later burned or buried:

After you come into the land to which I am bringing you, whenever you eat of the bread of the land, you shall present a donation to the Lord. From your first batch of dough you shall present a loaf as a donation; you shall present it just as you present a donation from the threshing-floor. Throughout your generations you shall give to the Lord a donation from the first of your batch of dough.

Numbers 15:18-21

The significance of unleavened bread is directly associated with the Passover meal, eaten in haste prior to the Exodus. And it is customary to accompany the Sabbath meal with two loaves of braided bread, challah, said to commemorate the double portion of manna the Israelites collected in the wilderness prior to the Sabbath:

Then the Lord said to Moses, 'I am going to rain bread from heaven for you, and each day the people shall go out and gather enough for that day. In that way I will test them, whether they will follow my instruction or not. On the sixth day, when they prepare what they bring in, it will be twice as much as they gather on other days.'

Exodus 16:4-5

God in the Qur'an is the provider from whom every creature receives provisions of life. It is God only who determines who will receive what and how much. The Qur'an says: 'Verily my Lord enlarges and restricts the Sustenance to such of his servants as He pleases: and nothing do ye spend in the least [in His cause] but He replaces it: for He is the Best of those who grant Sustenance' (34:39).

The Qur'an speaks of Mary and recounts how God provided her with fresh and delicious food from heaven that made the prophet Zakariya to wonder, and ask her, 'O Mary! Whence [comes] this to you?' She said: 'From Allah, for Allah provides sustenance to whom He pleases, without measure' (3:37). When the children of Israel were suffering from hunger and thirst, Moses prayed to God and God answered his prayers with food from heaven. The Qur'an says: '. . . we caused the clouds to comfort you with their shade, and sent down unto you manna and quails. [saying,] "Partake of the good things which We have provided for you as sustenance"' (2:57).

As we know, bread is vital to Christians.

All four Gospels contain accounts in which Jesus feeds multitudes with a few fishes and loaves of bread. After feeding them, Jesus instructs the crowd to work not for the 'food that perishes', but rather for the 'food that endures for eternal life' (John 6:27). The crowd remembers that God fed their ancestors in the desert with manna. Jesus reminds them that it was God, not Moses, from whom the manna came. Then he tells them: 'I am the bread of life. Whoever comes to me will never be hungry, and whoever believes in me will never be thirsty' (John 6:35). And bread is at the heart of the Lord's Prayer and the eucharist.

So, the simple roti reminds us that at the heart of our interfaith engagement is shared humanity, our need for sustenance and the desire for generosity. If God provides us with food then we have responsibilities to honour the gift, both in our rituals and sacrifices but also in our daily living. In all faiths there is an imperative to share food and to acknowledge that it is a divine gift to us. And in all faiths there is a call to generosity of spirit and to being mindful of the poor, the widowed and the hungry.

From the food offered freely at the Sikh Gurdwara as a langar meal,[1] to the collections of food made at church foodbanks, the imperative for this generosity with food and hospitality runs across the world of interfaith engagement. It continues to be the easiest way to make common cause with **people of varying religions and cultures. It also reminds us that, as people of faith, we have more in common than the** things that divide us. When politicians enjoin us to espouse 'British values', it is wise to be mindful of where these values are displayed in the everyday generosity of our varied faith communities.

I want to be clear: I am not saying that all faiths are the same, or all paths are the way to a shared heaven – although many do say this. And I am not implying that the Muslim understanding of Jesus is synonymous with the Christian. But what I do want the Christian community to acknowledge is that we have much to learn from other faith patterns of generosity and hospitality. When we lock the church coffee in the kitchen, we should note that the Sikhs give food away daily to the poor without counting the cost. And while we huddle around our Christmas dinner tables with our nearest and dearest, we are reminded **of true hospitality when the Eid meal is shared with communities simply because we are neighbours.**

The plain roti also reminds us of the tyrannies of food that exist in the world, the injustices of starvation in some societies whilst so much food is wasted in others. Bread is both the sign of our collective humanity and the judgement on us when so many live 'below the breadline'. But there are other tyrannies too. In Bradford there is the 'Square Chapati Club' in which young Asian girls get together to talk about the pressures on them to be married. The perfectly circular roti is a sign of a good wife, and of the ability to take care of a household. In a city where 70% of Asian marriages still have one partner born outside the UK, then the socio-political pressures that span the continents impinge on ordinary lives and households. Women are asking to have more say in what defines their human-ness. The politics **of food is** not simply a global issue **but also part** of our domestic reality.

Christian households are often **fragmented,** with each member eating **separately as** their varied lives do not **allow for a** common table. For the **Israelites, h**asty eating meant there **was no time** to put yeast into dough; **with our** modern pressures, it may **mean there** is no time even to put the **food in the** oven. Food becomes a **commodity** rather than a social necessity, **and the** consequent fragmentation of **relationships** can become an unhealthy, **daily phenom**enon.

Such fears about food reflect some **of our fears** about interfaith dialogue. **We might** not know what is in front **of us, we** might misinterpret social **expectations,** we might find that we **are out of o**ur depth or feel fearful for **our own we**ll-being. All these fears are **to be ackn**owledged and owned. They **are real.**

SO Time to name SOme fears about food:

 We might not know what is on our plate

 We might find food either too spicy or too bland

 We might be considered impolite or disrespectful because we don't know the etiquette of the meal

 We might fear the food will make us unwell

1. Food distribution as part of the Sikh discipline of faith.

The humble roti reminds us that the basis for all dialogue is a straightforward engagement with our shared identity as human beings, and that the Christian injunction to love our neighbour is an imperative to engage with people who are different from ourselves. The command to love our enemies, and pray for those who persecute us, is a sacrificial journey, one in which we are called to make ourselves vulnerable in the encounter with 'the other'. This can be both a delightful and a troubling journey.

And finally, the roti brings to mind that the Christian faith has its origins in the discourse of religious and cultural tensions. When Jesus broke bread, he was breaking both religious and cultural etiquette by taking the role of a woman at the Passover meal. And when Peter saw the great net of forbidden food coming down from heaven, he risked his self-identity as well as his gastronomic well-being at the house of Cornelius. Likewise, when Paul stood with the people of Corinth before the shrine to 'an unknown God', he was stepping across the barriers of religious certainties to engage with the discourse of our shared world, thereby risking his personal certitude for the expansion of the Kingdom.

Interfaith dialogue is not something invented in the UK in the light of multiculturalism. It is, and always has been, at the heart of our identity as Christians. Bread and relationship are at the centre of who we are as followers of Jesus. For us, as Christians, the simple roti denotes both our shared humanity with people of other faiths, and our distinctive belief in the incarnational, broken, eucharistic presence of God in the World in the person of Jesus.

Bread also reminds us, quite simply, that interfaith dialogue is primarily about friendship. It does not need to be a self-conscious effort to engage with doctrine and text; rather, it stems from the sharing of our life and food with people who are different from ourselves – on the bus, in the workplace, at the market. These incidental encounters form the 'glue' that binds communities together and enable us to relax in each other's multicultural company.

QUESTIONS TO ASK YOURSELF:

 Can I name five things which my faith has in common with another? Am I right?

 What is friendship? Is our church really friendly to people who are different from us?

What can I do to make my church, workplace or school more welcoming?

 How can I develop some practical ways to share food with people who are hungry? – e.g., a regular donation to a foodbank or gift aid to a homeless charity.

 Can I think of a friendship with someone really different from myself? How has this developed and enriched my life?

PRACTICAL things to do:

Have a bread-making session with some neighbours or try making round chapati!

Lead a worship session or school class on different sorts of bread and their origin in different cultures.

Have a chat with some of the stall holders at your local market.

Once a week dare yourself to do something out of your comfort zone.

Pray for opportunities to listen to other people's stories – and then really listen!

STORY: Jenny and Waheeda's story of friendship

I first met Waheeda when she became a colleague at Bradford College; we were part of a small team supporting vulnerable students and we quickly bonded over a shared love of cake and chocolate! We often spent break and lunch-times together, eating cake, getting to know each other, and becoming friends. We talked about anything and everything, discovering that we held many shared views on politics and social justice, and when our talk turned to our faith, we discovered that we held many shared views on that too – both passionately believing that God calls us to love our neighbour, and that we were each other's neighbour, despite having different faiths.

Both Waheeda and I suffered bereavements of close family members during our time at College, and it was during these times that I knew how important our friendship had become. Walking in to College having suffered a huge loss, it was her face I sought, and as her eyes welled up when we talked about what had happened, I knew that she understood completely. We both prayed for each other during these times, and I found this a huge comfort and support. I have learnt so much from Waheeda, about her own faith and about my own. Sometimes, if the office was empty, Waheeda would pray in the corner, and this led to conversations about why Muslims have set prayers five times a day, leading me to reflect on my own prayer life. I realised that very often I said to myself, 'Christians don't have set prayer, we can pray any time' and used this as an excuse to put off praying until later – often with the result that I hardly prayed at all!

These conversations led me to make sure I set aside set times for prayer in the mornings and evenings, which has helped develop my own relationship with God considerably. We don't work together any more, but we're still firm friends. Waheeda has been to my church, and I have visited her mosque, and we have both been together to speak to young people in schools about our friendship – we are both deeply committed to showing others that having a different faith need not be a barrier to friendship – in fact, it can enrich it more than you could ever imagine!

REMEMBER:

Different faiths have more in common than what separates them.

Sharing the things we have in common is not a compromise.

Friendship is the first step towards peace.

Recipe: Roti/Chapati (Makes about 6)

The Chapati Challenge! These are very easy to make and cook – and asking for the recipe was a bit like asking how to make mashed potato! But the trick is to master the art of making a round one . . . are you up to the challenge?

A large frying pan or griddle

300g chapati flour

(plain wholemeal wheat flour is the closest equivalent)

Water to mix

1. Mix water and flour into a dough.

2. Knead until the dough becomes elastic.

3. Leave in a bowl covered with a cloth, for 10 minutes.

4. Make small balls, roughly the size of a tennis ball. Roll out into a flat circle about 7" in diameter.

5. Heat pan for 30 seconds on high heat, then add rolled-out dough. Turn down to a medium heat and cook for about a minute each side, pressing the roti firmly as it cooks, using a cotton cloth or fish slice. Take care not to burn either yourself or the roti. Serve immediately.

Marinated Meat
when things feel a bit dry

The meat of choice in Indian, Pakistani or Bangladeshi cooking is very often either chicken or mutton. Each has particular benefits: chicken is easy to rear, and quick to cook, whereas mutton – the meat of a mature sheep – is a cheaper red meat, packed with flavour and character, that takes far longer in the pot to become tender. This makes it perfect for Asian cooking, where long, slow braising in rich, heavily-spiced sauces transforms older, tougher cuts of meat into meltingly tender delicacies, the spices working their way gently into the meat, mingling and mixing in the low heat of the pot.

Interfaith engagement leads to immersion: as we begin to dwell in multicultural contexts, we begin to soak up their cultures and flavours.

And as we do so, there are a number of questions that begin to surface, and these are mostly about the mix of faith, culture and identity. At one level it is churlish to want to separate these ingredients, as they are so intimately blended in the people around us, and in ourselves. On the other hand, it is in this process of discernment that we begin to move to deeper levels of understanding.

Our cultural and religious identities are a mix of personal histories and shared stories. This is manifest in ritual, architecture, music and writing, as well as in food and dress. This is often something that is more difficult to discern in ourselves than in others. What part of me is a specifically English Christian? How do I express being an English woman? What do I believe because of my family roots and what have I become because of the environment I inhabit? I know

that the answer to these questions lies in a complex mix of childhood socialising and cultural mores that have pervaded who I am and what I assume.

This mix of culture, faith and identity becomes all the more poignant in migrant communities. What can be changed without losing our identity? What is core to our being who we are? We hear this quandary expressed amongst the people of the exile in the Hebrew Bible, we hear of it in Paul's discourse with the Gentiles, and we continue to hear of it in Bradford amongst discussions concerning the hijab, faith education and religious customs. This is nothing new.

If we consider our culture to be the web of meanings we weave for ourselves, then there are some critical influences on how we weave that web. The first will be language, how we communicate with each other and what we choose to communicate, both verbally and using the written word. At its very basis is which language we choose for our vernacular and this will differ between the generations, and between the genders. In Bradford, where 70% of marriages still have one partner born overseas, first generation immigrants often never learn English at all. Subsequent generations will be increasingly multilingual, with original languages becoming more of a cultural choice. Interestingly, at my Urdu class at Bradford College, I am one of only three British heritage students, with the others in the class being of Asian heritage and learning Urdu for the first time in order to communicate more effectively with relatives and potential marriage partners.

If we are marinated in our spoken language, the cultural influence of language goes much further into the logic of the written word and the ways in which we engage

with text, both secular and religious. The English heritage of the Enlightenment encourages us to play with language. We are schooled to reason our way around arguments and discussions, we tell wry jokes that manipulate language in ways that sometimes only the British can understand!

Many Christians have also applied this approach to faith. We have reasoned with it and often reasoned ourselves out of it. We have engaged with biblical criticism as an academic discipline, or by critiquing the Bible in a group discussion. We are not fearful of pulling apart our religious texts – in fact, many of us find deeper and more important interpretations of our faith when we enter into the ambiguities of Scripture.

Whilst the concept of argument with God is a familiar occupation amongst the Jewish community, it would be much more controversial amongst Muslims, where obedience to the unchanging word is nearer the heart of their faith.

This web of identity, faith and culture is as complex as it is perplexing. Just when we begin to think that we understand those around us, we are shunted to a different depth of engagement. Just when we have a stereotype into which we can fit our neighbours, the ground shifts once again and we find it is not easy to sum up our experiences.

For instance, when we think we understand that wearing the hijab is a way of identifying with a place of 'home' and surmise that one day the next generation of British Muslims will become more 'Westernised', we discover that some young women born and bred in Bradford are choosing to wear traditional dress for a whole host of reasons, which are more of a response to Western Asian culture than they are to a land of origin that they have most probably never visited.

There is much to explore in the faith, identity, culture triangle. But the question I want to ask here is 'How does it make us feel?' – as this is a question most often overlooked by our culture which favours reason over feeling, and yet it is the place from which we most often react.

I want to explore some of my personal emotional response to the tugs between identity, faith and culture.

Others will have different experiences, but in naming our feelings I believe we can get to a more honest and eventually more creative engagement than when we just 'think' our way around the inter-religious landscape.

When I first moved from city-centre ministry in Liverpool to be the Team Leader at Touchstone in Bradford, I had the feeling of being on some sort of international exchange. If I went to the shops most people around me were speaking a language I couldn't understand and I didn't expect to have casual conversations with people along the way. In some respects this was a comfortable zone to be in, as it required little engagement with those around me. I had more trouble with finding myself in Yorkshire than pretending I was in Pakistan! I was happy enough but also felt myself becoming increasingly invisible.

This feeling of invisibility combined with the inability to communicate with many of my neighbours led to a growing **awareness of my 'inner racist'. I began to resent feeling like a st**ranger in **a strange land whil**st at the **same time enj**oying the **buzz and v**ariety of **my new** context.

After all, this is 'my country', a place where I have the right to feel at home. I became surprised both at my lack of tolerance and at my perceived inability to talk frankly about issues without a fear of being thought racist. I found that I was defending my Asian heritage neighbours to those outside Bradford whilst at the same time feeling stuck between two identities myself.

There was the on-going fluctuation between trying to be a good host to those who had migrated to this country, whilst increasingly feeling that I was the stranger. I began to muse about the difference between an exodus community and a community in exile and to search for my own story within the stories of migration all around me, and this led me into a deeper engagement with the complexity and nuances of my local community and my place within it.

These tensions between exile and exodus, between guest and host, between belonging and strangeness, are part of the shared process of interfaith engagement. As we are 'marinated' with a different culture, with the challenges of others' faiths and with their impact on our own identities, we move between polarities. And because these experiences challenge the nature of who we believe ourselves to be, we are also challenged to be genuinely ourselves in a context of diversities. Interfaith engagement doesn't just happen – it is both physical and emotional work.

- What is my culture and how do I express it every day?

- How has my personal history changed who I am? (It might be helpful to draw a timeline of your life story, or to use a piece of string, tying knots for significant life-changing events.)

- What assumptions do I make when I meet someone I don't know, and what influences my views?

- Am I a better host or guest?

- In my childhood/youth, was I part of any groups or gangs that had their own culture?

- Have I ever been excluded and how did it make me feel?

- Watch one of the following YouTube clips:
  What kind of Asian are you?
  www.youtube.com watch?v=DWynJkN5HbQ

  Go For an English
  www.youtube.com/watch?v=xdo79znnHl8

- Read and discuss one of the following books:
  Anita and Me by Meera Syal
  (Harper Perennial, 2004)
  The Boy with the Topknot
  by Sathnam Sanghera *(Penguin Books, 2009)*
  We are a Muslim, Please by Zaiba Malik
  (Windmill Books, 2011)

- Attend a group or activity that you've never been to before – or even a church that you think is not your scene.

- Ask someone of a different age from you what music they like, listen to it together and then share only positive thoughts!

- Go to an art exhibition exploring something you haven't thought of before.

Story:

After I had been in the city a few weeks, my neighbours called round to talk about some issues relating to the house. I made them a cup of tea and the father and son sat in my front room having a chat about this and that. It became obvious that they were hoping that we might be selling the house, as their family was expanding and they needed more space in the locality. I explained that we were not intending to sell the property but that, if we did, I would tell them straight away.

It became obvious during the conversation that the father had little English whilst the son was completely bilingual. From time to time during the conversation they would talk together in Punjabi which I didn't understand at all. I began to feel resentment that they were discussing things in a way I couldn't understand, and I began to feel protective about my position in the street.

I realised later that they had no intention of making me feel unwelcome. In fact, the father often comes round to cut my hedge and to tidy my garden in very natural acts of neighbourliness. When I find him sitting in my garden, I am no longer surprised and give him a wave out of the window. He clearly thinks that women should not do the gardening and I am quite happy to concede!

Recipe: Creamy Mutton Curry

About 1 kg mutton (diced shoulder)

350 ml whipping cream

1 tsp cayenne pepper

2 tbsp finely grated ginger

6 garlic cloves – crushed

1½ tsp salt

2 tbsp oil *(groundnut or corn)*

Whole spices:

    2 cinnamon sticks

    10 cardamom pods

2 bay leaves

1 large whole dried chilli

2 onions – sliced

1 tsp ground cumin

2 tsp ground coriander

½ tsp garam masala

Crushed pistachio nuts for topping

1. Put the diced mutton into a mixing bowl and add the whipping cream, cayenne pepper, ginger, crushed garlic and salt. Mix together well, cover and refrigerate for at least 4 hours, or preferably overnight.

2. Heat the oil in a large pan, add the bay leaves, cinnamon, cardamom pods and chilli.

3. When the chilli starts to darken, which should happen quickly, add the onions and fry until they start to brown.

4. Pour the meat and cream mixture into the pan, bring it to simmering point, cover and reduce the heat to a bare minimum.

5. Cook for 40 minutes to 1 hour, until the meat is nearly cooked, stirring occasionally to prevent the sauce from burning. Add a very small amount of water if needed.

6. Add to the mixture the cumin, coriander and garam masala and cook for a further 15 to 20 minutes, uncovered, then taste and add more salt if required. The sauce should be thick and rich, reduced and smooth.

7. Serve with crushed pistachio nuts on top.

REMEMBER:

🌶 We are all a mixture of culture, faith and identity.

🌶 Just when you think you can understand another point of view, you probably can't!

🌶 To feel excluded is to feel less than human.

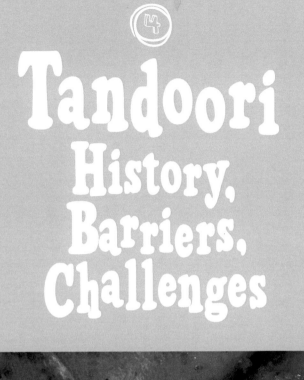

Tandoori
History, Barriers, Challenges

Whether you are just taking your first steps in interfaith engagement or have been at it for a long, long time, there will be times when things dry up.

That is, the good initial contacts that have been made are not followed through, or key people move on, or projects lose their funding or people are just too busy to make things happen. All these things can result in a sort of interfaith fatigue, along with the suspicion that you are doing all the running. Acknowledging that this is happening is both real and healthy.

There is also the negative pull of other voices. At a church service yesterday in which I had been talking positively about Touchstone's developing links with Pakistan and our push for interfaith engagement, an angry man challenged me by saying

'YOU aRE LiVing in a WORLD OF DELUSiOn RatheR than ReaLity'

and refused to talk any further. There is a prevalent attitude that interfaith engagement won't make any difference to the forces that are going to overcome us, and this is reinforced by media hype and increasing mistrust of 'the stranger'. And this increases the volume of our inner voices that tell us we are wasting our time or are in some way deluded.

And then there is the undertow of our imperialist and colonial past along with recent conflict history – a nagging sense that we are responsible for many of the dilemmas we now face and that it might simply be best to adopt a laissez-faire stance and simply muddle along in a nervous juxtaposition of communities. We can feel labelled as 'do-gooders' or 'God botherers' and tell ourselves that it might just be better to keep a low profile and not interfere.

This is the time to remind ourselves of the essential nature of interfaith, intercultural engagement. This is not an 'optional extra' for when we have got everything else sorted. And it is not

simply something that comes of necessity in multicultural areas. Interfaith, inter-religious engagement is essential for all of us, whether we live in Burnley or Bexhill, because we all live in the demography of migration and we are all challenged and changed by encountering faith systems and beliefs different from our own – be it by personal encounter or media influence. So how do we remain resilient and keep going?

There have been a number of studies, particularly in relation to children, that have investigated the nature of resilience and how to enable younger people to be both integrated and confident. These studies point to a number of helpful factors that help this engagement, and these can also be useful when we begin to think of 'faith resilience'.

THRee tiPS FOR Faith ResiLienCe:

1. Know where you fit into the story

Life gives us a story of who we are and where we belong. This sense of our own story is important in identifying who we are and how we relate to others. It will be a mixture of life events, family history, quirks of fate and serendipitous moments that changed our direction of travel. In time this turns into a well-worked narrative. For people of faith, this personal story also belongs within a bigger story, the story of the creation and redemption of the world. As Christians we also need to rehearse this narrative and be able to place ourselves within it as disciples of Jesus. On the whole, we are not particularly good at doing this. This

is partly because we operate out of an assumed 'norm'. Migrant communities are likely to have more of a sense of personal story being part of a faith story, because they may have more need to remember where they have come from and how they belong. But, on the whole, we white British Christians are a bit lazy. We are not accustomed to talking about our part in the overall journey of faith. So practising this is a good idea, working with biblical text, the Sunday sermon, novels and theological books, films . . . all these will help us practise saying who we are and what is key to our sense of belonging. When we have become better at doing this in the relative safety of a group of people we know, then we are more likely to be able to do it publicly amongst people of other faiths without either threatening or feeling threatened.

2. Work on good and sustaining relationships

Resilience is also enhanced by being part of a group of people who are committed to each other in deep and honest relationships. There is no better place to do this than a church – so why are we so bad at it? If we are expecting to be able to enter into deep conversation with people of other faiths, then we need to practise with people of our own faith. Christianity is not a monochrome religion – there are a whole variety of opinions and interpretations within every denomination and some significant points of disagreement.

Recently the Methodist Church talked of re-connecting with Wesley's injunction to be a 'fellowship of controversy'. That is, we pledged ourselves to disagree well! What better way to learn to be honest and open and yet to be able to hold fast to our non-negotiables? Disagreeing well is a sign of a faith community coming of age, and engaging maturely with controversial matters. I wonder how we could learn to practise this amongst other Christians in such a way that our relationships are emboldened?

3. Set good boundaries

Another pointer in the journey towards faith resilience is a mature ability to negotiate and uphold safe boundaries. It is much simpler for us to operate in separate communities in which we are not 'invaded' by the thoughts and insights of others. But how dull is that!

Positive engagement with people of other faiths needs us to have the skills to engage and disengage, to meet and to reflect, to create a safe enough space to be true to who we are and to listen to the experiences of others with respect and compassion. This is an intentional process, and bearing in mind we cannot be all things to all people, or understand the whole of another faith or culture, we need to be able to target where our energy is best spent. Would we like to engage in community issues, with women's groups, in the political forum or with educational reform? Channelling our interfaith engagement to one or two focused places will enable a deeper involvement and companionship around things held in common, rather than an overwhelming sense of the whole thing being much too big.

This ability to be resilient is not to make us impervious to people of other faiths – it is not about being Teflon-coated. On the contrary, it is about helping us to be strong enough in ourselves and in our own faith to feel that we have confidence to be who we are in relation to others. It's about getting real to what is possible and doing it really well. It also has within it a view of mission that is firm in what we believe, yet not overwhelmed. It involves a respect for others without having to be the same as them, and the notion that we can have a strong faith of our own without compromising that of someone else. It will also help us to get unstuck when things feel dry and difficult. In this way we may be enabled to stop skimming the surface of interfaith engagement and to deepen our understanding of both ourselves and others.

So, to become more faith resilient it is necessary for us to know where we fit into our personal and our faith stories, to work on a few sustaining relationships and to set good boundaries. These simple parameters can help us to feel less overwhelmed and more able to make deeper alliances with our neighbours of different faiths.

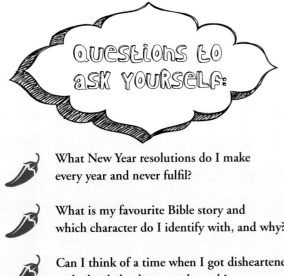

QUESTIONS TO ASK YOURSELF:

What New Year resolutions do I make every year and never fulfil?

What is my favourite Bible story and which character do I identify with, and why?

Can I think of a time when I got disheartened and what helped me get through?

Who do I go to for support and what helps me sustain a positive attitude?

Are there any relationships that I want to change or re-negotiate?

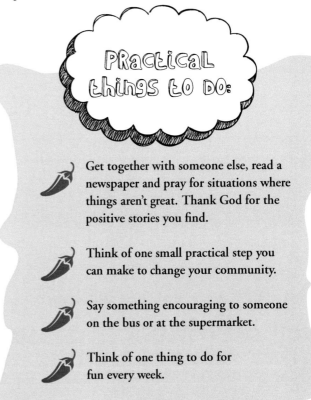

PRACTICAL things to do:

Get together with someone else, read a newspaper and pray for situations where things aren't great. Thank God for the positive stories you find.

Think of one small practical step you can make to change your community.

Say something encouraging to someone on the bus or at the supermarket.

Think of one thing to do for fun every week.

Recipe: Tandoori Chicken

To make your own tandoori spice mix:

½ tsp red chilli powder
1 tsp turmeric
2 tsp dried fenugreek leaves
4 tsp paprika powder
1 tblsp coriander powder
2 tblsp ground cumin
2 tblsp garam masala

Mix all the ingredients above using a whisk or spoon and store the mixture in an airtight container. The spice mix should stay fresh for about 5 weeks.

For the chicken:

1kg chicken drumsticks, skinned
pinch salt
1 lemon, juice only
250g/9oz plain yoghurt
2 tbsp tandoori spice mix

1. Using a small, sharp knife make deep incisions into the chicken flesh. Put the chicken into a bowl. Sprinkle over the salt and the lemon juice, and rub into the chicken thoroughly.

2. Mix the yoghurt and tandoori spice in a bowl. Pour the marinade onto the chicken and rub into the flesh. Cover with clingfilm and place in the fridge overnight or at least 4 hours before cooking to allow flavours to infuse.

3. Preheat the grill to high.

4. Remove the drumsticks from the tandoori mixture and shake off any excess. Grill for 20 minutes, turning regularly, or until richly burnished and the chicken is cooked through.

For the dip:

2 tbsp plain yoghurt
pinch salt
pinch sugar
2 tsp mint sauce
1 green chilli, deseeded, sliced (optional)

Place all of the ingredients into a food processor and blend until smooth. Serve alongside the chicken drumsticks.

STORY:

A small project in Cornwall made rugs together and had conversations together; this is what they wrote of the experience:

We met in a children's centre in Truro and the group consisted mainly of mothers with young children. We had one Muslim lady, four Christian ladies and one agnostic lady.

The process of making a design was wonderful – sharing stories, finding our common qualities of wisdom – and the design just appeared out of nothing. We have been working hard since. The group has really come together.

Our faith communities have been under strain since the shootings in Paris[2] and making the rug has been really supportive. Sharing stories and learning practical skills feels like an ancient rite of passage for women and has been very healing.

2. At the offices of the *Charlie Hebdo magazine* in January 2015.

REMEMBER:

🌶 Interfaith engagement has ups and downs.

🌶 If the big picture is too daunting, do something small, and do it well.

🌶 Listening is the best way to honour stories.

Vindaloo- when things get heated!

The vindaloo has its roots in the south of India, in the seafaring states of Kerala and particularly Goa, the areas formerly colonised by the Portuguese.

The Portuguese brought with them 'carne de vinha d'alhos', a traditional feast dish of meat cooked in red wine with garlic. The vindaloo represents the collision of Portugal's culinary heritage with that of India. Carne de vinha d'alhos gained some spices, a lot of chilli and, somewhere long the way, the wine gave way to vinegar, and the vindaloo emerged.

The average British curry house does the vindaloo a great disservice. It's presented as the ultimate fiery dish, a curry laced with so much chilli that it's almost inedible, a world away from the original dish of gently spiced and marinated meat, sweet with palm sugar, sour with vinegar.

There are moments when an overzealous chilli can grab our tonsils and cause a gastronomic meltdown. This is true of cultural relationships too. International politics, local relationships, family feuds and the increasing strains of poverty all add fuel to argument and civil disquiet. In addition, there are those factions and organisations whose purpose is to be inflammatory. So let's think first about the factors that can spark problems and then how to limit both their likelihood and their damage.

The first thing a fire needs is kindling, fuel, something to ignite.

This is the day to day, drip drip of intercultural anxiety and rising tension. This is often so routine that we no longer notice it, but our newspapers, TV and radio programmes provide a source of continuing anxiety. Added to this, certain neighbourhoods embody this anxiety, and nowhere more than Bradford. The reality of this is often quite contrary to the perception, which is why it is increasingly important for non-mixed areas to be educated and informed.

What is true, however, is that places like Bradford have multiple indices of deprivation which make integration and understanding more challenging than in many other places. The social demography of the urban working-class poor becomes increasingly challenged when those who are upwardly mobile move away. Resentments build and grievances are often blamed on the incomers. This is not a simple matter of white resenting Asian, but has the complexity of inter-Muslim tensions, Asian and white both resenting Eastern European, and so on. Our fear of the stranger is multi-faceted and complex and we manage it (or not) on a daily basis.

These various resentments in a context of depression and multiple deprivation comprise the fuel ready to be ignited by a random spark. But not all sparks are random; some are planned. Northern mill towns and other multicultural areas are relentlessly targeted by right-wing organisations such as the English Defence League (EDL) and Britain First. And the trouble with this is that some of what they say feeds the everyday fears of ordinary people trying to make sense of their changing neighbourhoods. Behind this can be a more dangerous and sinister agenda.

On the other hand, there is the fear, real or otherwise, of increasing radicalisation amongst

Asian communities. It only takes a few passionate young people to join in the fight against the perceived 'norms' of the West and it is assumed that everyone wearing a hijab or attending Friday prayers represents a possible terrorist threat. Government rhetoric can reinforce this fear and community tensions rise. Local communities can become tinder dry.

All it then takes is for some sort of ignition and sparks can happen for all sorts of reasons.

In Bradford this year, the tensions in the city rose noticeably towards the end of Ramadan as the days were long and Muslim families had a long wait through hot weather to break their fast. But local tensions can also rise because of increased police activity in neighbourhoods, the activities of right-wing organisations, or international tensions. In these days of almost instant dissemination of world news, global politics penetrate quickly into local areas. So, added to the stresses of Ramadan this year, came news of increased hostility in the Middle East and Gaza. Whether it is a racist comment in the corner shop or pub, or an international crisis stirring people to action, inflammatory situations can arise quickly if there is already enough anger to fuel them.

As with any fire, the blaze will only continue if there is enough oxygen. We live in a context in the UK that gives a lot of oxygen to intercultural, interfaith tensions. The beheading of a citizen in London or the murder of a solider is no longer described as an atrocity perpetrated by someone out of their mind, but is more often than not given a faith or racial label – Asian man kills woman, Muslim leader incites hatred. Giving airtime to racial or faith stereotypes continues to confirm prejudice in communities, confirming our worst fears and instilling a sense of threat which fuels the fire. The reaction to this is often to batten down the hatches and to withdraw from engagement. The reaction of the police and others tasked with enforcing civil obedience may well be to 'put the lid on it'. This is always a last and emergency measure. What is really important is to find safe enough spaces to talk about the issues that surround us, before the sparks fly.

Once conflict has erupted, it is very difficult to extinguish it.

Conflict resolution experts advise us that there is a point of no return at which further intervention becomes no longer possible until the flames have died down of their own accord. However, conflict does have a recognisable

trajectory and there are strategies that are possible before the 'no-return point' has been reached. The conventional thinking on conflict prevention in local communities is to push towards social cohesion. Social cohesion is a term that describes the number of relationships within communities that can form a bond in times of trouble. Whilst social cohesion policies still have some credence, what is more important is that this bond of relationships is deep enough and wide enough and honest enough to face conflict with real insight: that is, that community relationships have got beyond the 'curry and quiche' mentality and are a network that enables people to talk about deep issues in safe places.

Let's take a real example. The EDL post on their website that they are planning a trip to Bradford. The police advise that as many people as possible should stay away from the city centre. The City Council promotes alternative venues and activities on that day. The youth service organises trips away from the city centre. The churches liaise with the Council, the Council for Mosques, the Gurdwara and Hindu Temple and put peacemakers on the street as a quiet presence on the day. It is important that all these people already know and trust each other in advance of the day and that, where the agendas clash, there is appropriate space to negotiate a mutually acceptable strategy. Only ongoing, quiet, relational and honest community engagement can avoid panic stations when a crisis hits.

In the days after the last visit of the EDL the faith leaders also organised a time of prayer to reclaim the streets and for the communities to settle back again into their everyday lives. They were also able to issue joint statements to the press that took some of the oxygen away from the rhetoric of angst. Holding our nerve in times of crisis is a sign of a city coming of age and being mature enough to manage conflict with resilience and trust.

Instead of community cohesion and integration, maybe it would be more helpful to talk of a city in search of integrity? Integrity offers a way of holding disparate communities within a creative rather than a destructive tension. It implies the ability to talk through difference rather than meet it head on. It is true that there will always be struggles between people of differing culture and faith but, as John Wesley noted, we need to be able to live within a fellowship of controversy. That is, we need to be mature enough to name our differences in honest and open spaces so that we can de-escalate violence when it is provoked among us.

Taking the oxygen out of the air that conflict breathes is a day to day community activity. It may be of a greater urgency in multicultural city centres than in a small village somewhere, but we all need to be alert. To challenge hostility towards incomers and to resist the voices that claim the high ground is a Christian prerogative, because we are called always and everywhere to love our enemies and pray for those who persecute us, either in our own culture or in the many cultures that challenge and enhance our community's life.

Questions to ask Yourself:

Blessed are the peacemakers – how can I be a better peacemaker?

How can I stay calm and be less defensive when faced with conflict in my family or community?

What makes me angry? When I am angry, who do I blame?

Who or what are my enemies?

Is there such a thing as righteous anger? What positive things could I do to channel it?

Practical things to do:

Watch the film Pray the Devil back to Hell.

Find other groups working together for your community, and see how to support them.

Make a list of faith and community leaders and get to know them and support them.

Keep praying for peace and being a peaceful presence.

Make safe spaces for people to calm down; open the church for a vigil.

Find ways to work with your youth organisations to name issues and encourage peaceful strategies.

DAILY nEWS

CITY COMES TOGETHER IN SHOW OF HARMONY AHEAD OF PROTEST

Hundreds of people in communities across the Bradford district came together last night to express their solidarity ahead of today's planned demonstrations by far-right and left-wing protesters.

The peace vigil, organised by the group Bradford Together, was designed to show the world a positive side to Bradford before members of the English Defence League, countered by supporters of Unite Against Fascism, descend on the city. Representatives of religious groups spoke to a crowd of about 300-strong in Jacob's Well car park to highlight the links between different communities in the city.

Many people wore green ribbons, provided by supporters of campaign group Bradford Women for Peace, who held their own vigil in Ivegate earlier in the day.

Members of the crowd wrote messages of support for the city on a peace wall and a tree of peace bearing further messages was also on display.

The vigil finished with 'We Shall Overcome', a protest song that became the unofficial anthem of the US civil rights movement in the 1960s and has since been adopted internationally as a song of peace.

Also at the vigil was Helen Johnston, 47, of Halifax. She said: 'I have worked in Bradford for more than 20 years and I think it's a wonderful place and the people are wonderful too. I don't like it when anything threatens that so I have come to show I support Bradford and Bradford people.'

Bradford Women for Peace yesterday draped lime green banners, giant bows and peace ribbon across the city to leave 'a trail of peace' ahead of the demonstrations.

Recipe: Lamb Vindaloo

REMEMBER:

🌶 Peace is born out of existing friendships.

🌶 Anger is not wrong – it just needs to be used in creative, not destructive, ways.

🌶 Praying for peace is vocational and essential.

1.3 kg boneless lamb shoulder cut into roughly 1¾" chunks
100ml red wine vinegar
2 tbsp sunflower oil
2 tsp sea salt flakes
500g potatoes, peeled and cut into roughly 1" pieces

For the sauce:
125ml sunflower oil
4 onions, 3 finely sliced and 1 chopped
6 garlic cloves, roughly chopped
3 long red chillies (do not deseed), roughly chopped
25g fresh root ginger, peeled, roughly chopped
1 tbsp English mustard powder
1 tbsp ground cumin
1 tbsp ground coriander
1 tbsp ground paprika
2 tsp ground turmeric
2 tsp cayenne pepper
1 tsp ground cinnamon
2 tsp sea salt flakes
2 bay leaves

1. It's worth spending time trimming off the hard lumps of fat from the lamb, as lamb can be very fatty. Thoroughly combine the vinegar, oil and salt, then add the lamb, ensuring the marinade coats all the meat. Cover with cling film and chill for 2 hours.

2. Preheat the oven to 180°C/350°F/Gas mark 4.

3. Note: do not use all the onions at this stage! Heat 3 tbsps of oil and gently cook the sliced onions over a low heat for 15 minutes, stirring occasionally, until lightly browned and soft.

4. For the curry paste: while cooking the onions, put the remaining chopped onions, garlic, chillies, ginger, mustard powder, cumin, coriander, paprika, turmeric, cayenne pepper and cinnamon in a food processor and blend to a puree.

5. Stir the paste into the cooked onions. Add 2 tblsps of oil and cook for 5 minutes to draw out the flavours of the spices until the mixture thickens and begins to colour. Tip the mixture into casserole dish.

6. Drain the lamb, keeping the marinade in a dish. Add lamb to pan and heat in 2 tbsps of oil. Seal the meat by frying the lamb in batches over a medium heat until lightly browned. Use extra oil if necessary. Add lamb to the casserole.

7. Add the remaining marinade to the casserole and add 500ml of water. Add salt and bay leaves. Cover the surface of the curry with a piece of greaseproof paper to absorb some of the excess fat, then cover with lid. Put in the pre-heated oven for 45 minutes.

8. After 45 minutes, add the potato chunks, replace the greaseproof paper, and cook for a further hour, until the lamb and potatoes are tender. Season to taste. Best served with warmed naans or rice – and some natural yoghurt to counteract the heat!

Chai Hospitality

Roll into a station on a packed train anywhere across India or Pakistan, and there's a good chance that a chai wallah will swing into action, wielding a huge stack of small, simple unglazed terracotta cups and a huge pot of steaming tea.

For a rupee or two, a cup of chai will find its way through the train window to you, a small refreshment gulped down in a few sips, following which the terracotta cup is released back through the window from which it came, to join the smashed remains of countless other such cups decorating the side of the track.

We live on a small, green island and we can often think of migration in terms of a pirate attack and easily slip into the language of 'repelling all boarders', rather than seeing the 'Earth as the Lord's and all the people therein' (see Psalm 24). Clearly the migration of peoples across the globe has impact on local identities and economies, but nations have never been static and people have always moved and sometimes been encouraged to move, through economic or social necessity.

From earliest times these migrations have meant that people have encountered different cultural and faith perspectives. From Abram, the wandering Aramean, to the present migrations in multicultural Britain, we hear of the struggles and joys that such cultural and religious encounters have engendered, how they have challenged indigenous identities as well as brought the rich heritage and insights of other places. Interfaith dialogue is nothing new, and we are in a continuous process of engagement, struggle and learning.

Maybe this is no more clearly symbolised than by the simple cup of tea, or chai.

At a church gathering recently, we were admonished by a lady in the kitchen for suggesting they might have Earl Grey. 'Oh, no,' she rebuked us, 'we only have English tea here!' Tea after all is no more English than a plate of chips (potatoes came from America, didn't they?) and in the simple cuppa lies the rich blend of all that has enriched our lives since our ancestors set sail for Asia.

Tea also represents our colonial past, the reason why we were in India and Sri Lanka, the multimillion-pound businesses that have flourished and provide trade opportunities across the globe. And we are all a bit sniffy about tea – whether the milk goes in before or after the hot liquid, whether we use leaves or bags, whether we boil the milk in a pan with the tea leaves and add lashings of sugar, whether we add cardamom. Tea represents not only our cultural histories but also our local identities. Nobody makes tea quite as well as we do!

But, more importantly, tea is a very basic sign of our hospitality one to another.

But, more importantly, tea is a very basic sign of our hospitality one to another. Across the world, the first words of welcome in many households are 'Would you like some tea?' and, although what we actually receive at the end of the boiling process may be as varied as the people that have brewed it, the simple cup of tea denotes a welcome that is irrespective of creed, colour or culture.

The word 'hospitality' derives from the same root as the word 'host' and is the exact opposite of the word 'xenophobia' or fear of the stranger. To be hospitable means that we are prepared to receive strangers into the intimate surroundings of our own home and to treat them as if they were family. And to be a good guest is to be able to receive what is offered and to use the occasion to start a conversation.

This back and forth between host and guest, strangeness and hospitality, is at the core of all faith traditions, because to be hospitable is the first step towards peace building, between families, communities and nations. Sharing food together we become more vulnerable to each other and to the way in which we do things. We become more open to another's understanding and interpretation of the world, and we begin to expand our horizons to see that we are not always right and that our way is not the only way of doing things.

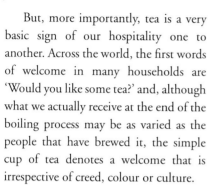

Jesus knew this when he broke bread with his mixed-up bunch of disciples.

Sharing food was central to who they were and who they were becoming together.

And in the eucharist this radical hospitality extends beyond the confines of those in Jesus' inner circle of friends to include the whole world. This does not necessarily mean that we are all called to sign up to one faith position – rather that we, like the first followers of Jesus, are called into fellowships of controversy. By definition we don't believe things because we think they are wrong, we believe because we trust there is truth in the revelation that has come to us. To be hospitable does not mean that we have to agree with everyone else, but rather that we are prepared to be open to another's offer of humanity at our homes and tables.

Interfaith dialogue is not a sort of fusion food, where we all have a little taste of someone else's repast; rather, it is an invitation to sit down to a hearty meal in someone else's traditional way. In my experience, what most Muslims **expect of us** is that we try to be good **Christians,** that we are true to our own **faith and att**empt to live it out in the **day to day str**uggles of our lives at work **and within** our families. They probably **already know** a great deal about Jesus **and will resp**ect our belief that we have **a different a**nd living relation with God **through him.** It's OK for us to explain **this and fo**r them to disagree – this **doesn't mak**e our faith any less or theirs

any more powerful. The power lies in the conversation, in the disagreement, in the friendship and fundamentally in the hospitality of being accepted into another's home, both physically and emotionally.

Eventually the notion of hosts and guests will diminish, and we will simply have friends of other faiths and cultures than our own. In this we have nothing to fear and through this encounter a new understanding can begin to dawn on the world, despite the forces of international politics. But we mustn't be deluded into thinking this is something optional for when we've got everything else sorted out. The radical hospitality of inter-religious engagement is crucial stuff. Never has there been such a perceived threat to world peace with such overt religious labels associated with it. And never has there been more need to be wisely engaged in increasing interfaith understanding.

We know only too well what happens when things go wrong, in Syria, Iraq, Pakistan, Ethiopia, Bosnia. When people are labelled simply by their religious heritage, then there can be excuses for ethnic cleansing and holocaust. To follow Jesus is to follow a man who was born into just such a conflict and was ultimately crucified because his beliefs, convictions, and his very being were too threatening to those around him. We are called to live out just such strong gentleness. To be resilient in our faith through remembering our part in the Jesus story. To be people of integrity who can hold it together when things fall apart around us. To put our bodies where our beliefs are, just as Jesus did. It is a crucial engagement, whether we live in multicultural areas or in seemingly monocultural communities. It is only open hearts that will ever change the world.

Questions to ask yourself:

🌶 Hospitality means 'love of the stranger'. Who could I share food with – someone I've never asked round before?

🌶 Do I find it easy or difficult to talk to people I don't know?

🌶 Can I make a list of different forms of hospitality, and what ways do I feel are most possible for me?

Practical things to do:

🌶 Put on a church event for people in the community.

🌶 Have a street party.

🌶 Find out about groups that help asylum seekers and refugees in your area and see what help they need.

🌶 Collect recipes and make a recipe book.

🌶 Have a youth group meal for the church or put on a talent show to help a community cause.

🌶 Look out for 'Sold' signs on houses or flats near you and go round with a welcome card.

Story:

Mr Khan came to Bradford in 1967 to join his father who was already here working in the mills. He started work at the Karachi restaurant, which was then owned by his uncle but it took him a while to get used to the language, the clothes, the living accommodation and, of course, the climate!

Initially, white Bradfordians were suspicious of the different tastes and dishes on offer at the Karachi, and customers were mainly other Pakistani immigrants. Gradually, however, their reputation grew and Mr Khan recalls a time when queues would form at 5am, as people came out of the night clubs wanting their curry before heading home.

Mr Khan and his staff have taught their customers how to eat with their hands, and responded to changing tastes, and now the majority of their customers are white Bradfordians – and the curry served is hotter and spicier than when they first opened.

Such is the lasting reputation of the Karachi that many of their original customers still regularly eat here, bringing with them their children and grandchildren. Indeed, as we sat talking to Mr Khan, the man on the next table confirmed that he had been coming every week since 1964! No wonder, then, that Rick Stein commended the restaurant when he visited as part of his 'Food Heroes' series.

Recipe: Chai or Deli, meaning tea

REMEMBER:

🌶 Hospitality means welcoming strangers.

🌶 It's a Christian calling, not a lifestyle option.

🌶 Simple is good!

Thanks to Mr Khan from the Karachi for his hospitality – and for sharing the secrets of this authentic drink.

1 cup milk
1 tea bag
½ tsp sugar

1. Put milk into a pan with the tea bag.

2. Boil the milk with tea bag for 4 minutes.

3. Take off the boil, remove tea bag and add sugar. Try a sprinkle of salt, cardamom and/or extra sugar to taste.

Suggestions for further reading, viewing and thinking

Want to find out more?

You could try these books:

A Heart Broken Open by Ray Gaston — Wild Goose Publications, 2009

Celebrating Difference, Staying Faithful by Alan Wingate — Darton, Longman and Todd, 2012

Dear Abdullah: Eight Questions Muslim People ask about Christianity by Robert Scott — Intravarsity Press, 2011

Interfaith Encounter by Alan Race — SCM Press, 2001

My Neighbor's Faith ed. Jennifer Howe Peace, Or N. Rose and Gregory Mobley — Orbis Books, 2012

The Bible and Other Faiths by Ida Glaser — Langham Global Library, 2012

Together and Different ed. Malcolm Torry and Sarah Thorley — Canterbury Press, 2008

You could read these reports:

- **Building Good Relations with People of Different Faiths and Beliefs**,
  The Inter Faith network for the United Kingdom
  (available at http://www.interfaith.org.uk/publications/all-publications/doc_download/2-building-good-relations-between-people-of-different-faiths-and-beliefs-code)

- **Generous Love: the truth of the Gospel and the call to dialogue**,
  Anglican Communion Network for Inter Faith Concerns
  (available at http://www.anglicancommunion.org/media/18910
  generous_love_a4_with_foreward.pdf?subject=Inter+faith)

- **Presence and Engagement – The churches' task in a
  multi-faith society**, Inter Faith Consultative Group
  (available at https://www.churchofengland.org/media/36607/presence.pdf

You could watch these films:

- East is East (1999)
- The Imam and the Pastor (2008)
- Pray the Devil Back to Hell
  (2008, about Christian and Muslim women in Sierra Leone)

- West is West (2010)
- Keeping the Faith (2000, comedy)
- Yasmine (2014)
- Of Gods and Men (2010)

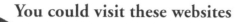

You could visit these websites

Churches Together in Britain and Ireland	www.ctbi.org.uk
Hindu Christian Forum	www.hinduchristianforum.co.uk
Inter Faith UK	www.interfaith.org.uk
Muslims Ask, Christians Answer	http://aam.s1205.t3isp.de/?L=1
Suffolk Inter-Faith Resource	www.sifre.org.uk
The Council of Christians and Jews	www.ccj.org.uk
Touchstone	www.touchstone-bradford.org.uk
World Council of Churches	www.oikoumene.org

You could read these stories

Anita and Me by Meera Syal	Harper Collins, 2004
Brick Lane by Monica Ali	Doubleday, 2003
We are a Muslim, Please by Zaiba Malik	Windmill Books, 2011
The Boy with the Topknot by Sathnam Sanghera	Penguin, 2009

For younger people

8 and under

- **Making Friends** and **My Best Friend** both by Nicola Call and Sally Featherstone — *for the very young, friendship.*
  Featherstone Education, 2014 & 2013

- **My Friend Jamal** by Anna McQuinn and Ben Frey — *a friendship between Jamal (a Muslim) and Joseph.*
  Annick Press, 2008

- **New Friend, Old Friends** by Julia Jarman
  Shazia has moved to the UK from Pakistan and must manage the relationships with new friends and family.
  Andersen Press, 2014

- **The Colour of Home** by Mary Hoffman and Karin Littlewood
  Hassan is a refugee in the UK from Somalia, adjusting to a very different life.
  Frances Lincoln Children's Books, 2003

- **Wasim and the Champ** by Chris Ashley
  Football, white against Asian resolved with the arrival of the Champ (others in this series also).
  Frances Lincoln Children's Books, 2011

8 to 11-ish

- **Christophe's Story** and **Armel's Revenge** both by Nicki Cornwell
  Christophe and his family flee Rwanda to the UK.
  He is expected to look after the next new boy.
  Frances Lincoln Children's Books, 2011

- **My Friend the Enemy** by Dan Smith
  World War II moral dilemma when German plane is shot down over Britain and airman is injured.
  Chicken House, 2013

- **Nadine Dreams of Home** by Bernard Ashley   Barrington Stoke Ltd, 2014
  Settling into the UK from Goma is difficult when you don't know what happened to your Dad .

- **Secret Friends** by Elizabeth Laird   Hodder Children's Books, 2002

Older

- **Does My Head Look Big in This?** by Randa Abdel-Fattah   Marion Lloyd Books, 2006
  Being a 16-year-old Muslim girl in Melbourne, funny.

- **My Sister Lives on the Mantelpiece** by Annabel Pitcher   Orion Children's Books, 2013
  Jamie, his Dad and sister move to the Lake District after his twin sister is killed in a terrorist attack. Brilliant at looking at all the issues from various family members' angles. Surprisingly funny, moving, excellent.

- **Secrets of the Henna Girl** by Sufiya Ahmed   Puffin, 2012
  Similar storyline to Ten Things..., being 16 in the UK with strict Muslim parents.

- **Ten Things I Hate About Me** by Randa Abdel-Fattah   Marion Lloyd Books, 2007
  Conflict between being a teenage Australian and a good Muslim girl.

More general living with differences:

- **Noughts and Crosses** by Malorie Blackman   Corgi Childrens, 2006
  Dystopian novel for older readers.

- **Out of Shadows** by Jason Wallace   Andersen Press, 2010
  Set in post-apartheid Zimbabwe.

- **The Diddakoi** by Rumer Godden   Macmillan Children's Books, 2013
  Struggles of a young Romany gypsy.

- **Have You Seen Who's Just Moved in Next Door to Us?** by Colin McNaughton   Walker, 2013
  For younger readers, very visual.

Finally, there is a very good book that may be of interest called:

- **Really, Really Big Questions about Faith** by Julian Baggini,   Kingfisher, 2011
  which looks at aspects of faith from all angles.

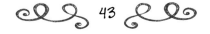

PS: How to make Samosa!

REMEMBER:

Interfaith engagement is for everyone, wherever you live.

There's no such thing as an expert, but there's also no excuse for ignorance

This is about human beings of differing cultures learning to be together – it can be fun and will increase awareness of your self and of what is important about your faith and world.

And of course by now you will have realised there are lots of recipes and varieties of this tasty dish – here's a vegetarian one!

3 tbsp vegetable oil

½ tsp mustard seeds

60g chopped onion

1 tsp finely chopped ginger

60g frozen peas

1 tbsp ground coriander

1 tsp ground cumin

¼ tsp red chilli powder

½-¾ tsp garam masala

juice of half a lemon

salt to taste

splash of water

600g potatoes, peeled, boiled until soft and crushed into large lumps

4 tbsp chopped coriander leaves

1 packet ready-made filo pastry

5 tbsp melted butter, for brushing

1. Heat the oil in a small non-stick pan and fry the mustard seeds for about ten seconds, or until they begin to splutter.

2. Add the onion and ginger and cook for 2-3 minutes over a high heat. Add the peas, stir well and add the spices, mango powder, salt and a splash of water or lemon juice.

Cook for 1-2 minutes, then add the potatoes and coriander and cook for a further 2-3 minutes. Taste and adjust the seasoning.

3. Preheat the oven to 200C/400F/Gas 6.

4. Unroll the pastry and cover with cling film and a damp tea towel. Peel off one piece and keep the rest covered so that it doesn't dry out. Lay the pastry sheet flat on a clean surface and brush with melted butter. Fold in one third of the pastry lengthways towards the middle. Brush again with the butter and fold in the other side to make a long triple-layered strip.

5. Place one rounded teaspoon of the filling mixture at one end of the strip, leaving a 1" border. Take the right corner and fold diagonally to the left, enclosing the filling and forming a triangle. Fold again along the upper crease of the triangle. Keep folding in this way until you reach the end of the strip. Brush the outer surface with more butter. Place on a baking sheet, and cover while you make the rest of the samosas. Sprinkle over a few sesame seeds, if using.

6. Bake in the centre of the oven for 30-35 minutes, or until golden and crisp, turning halfway through the cooking time.

7. To serve, place the samosas on a large serving plate and ask some friends round to 'share curry for Heaven's sake'!